Percy Hetherington Fitzgerald

The Romance of the English Stage

In Two Volumes. Vol. II

Percy Hetherington Fitzgerald

The Romance of the English Stage
In Two Volumes. Vol. II

ISBN/EAN: 9783744696425

Printed in Europe, USA, Canada, Australia, Japan

Cover: Foto ©Thomas Meinert / pixelio.de

More available books at **www.hansebooks.com**

THE ROMANCE

OF

THE ENGLISH STAGE.

BY

PERCY FITZGERALD, M.A., F.S.A.,

AUTHOR OF THE 'LIFE OF GARRICK,' 'THE KEMBLES,' ETC.

IN TWO VOLUMES.

Vol. II.

LONDON:
RICHARD BENTLEY & SON, NEW BURLINGTON STREET.
Publishers in Ordinary to Her Majesty.
1874.

CONTENTS.

CHAPTER I.
"THE ILL-FATED MOSSOP" ... 1

CHAPTER II.
LOVE AND DEATH UPON THE STAGE ... 19

CHAPTER III.
THE IRELAND FORGERIES ... 76

CHAPTER IV.
MRS. ROBINSON ... 96

CHAPTER V.
GEORGE FREDERICK COOKE ... 158

CHAPTER VI.
ELLISTON ... 204

CHAPTER VII.
GERALD GRIFFIN ... 265

CHAPTER VIII.
THE YOUNG ROSCIUS ... 299

THE ROMANCE OF THE STAGE.

CHAPTER I.

"THE ILL-FATED MOSSOP."*

AMONG the actors with which the stage is crowded, a most interesting figure is that of Mossop, of whom perhaps little more is known, by the average light reader, than his name and rivalry with Garrick. His unfamiliar story must attract sympathy—such sympathy as is extended to the proud, rude nature that resents neglect, but disdains to complain. It is one of the most painful histories connected with the stage.

The success of Garrick, an officer's son, and the vast interest excited in the legitimate drama, seemed to draw a number of clever young men, of good birth and connections, to the stage. A long list in particular could be made out of the

* Born 1729, died 1773.

graduates and students of Trinity College, Dublin, who adopted the profession. Distinguished among these was Henry Mossop, the son of a clergyman, himself intended for the church, but who could not resist the attraction of the " headlights " the now familiar footlights then not existing. He made his appearance in 1749, as Zanga, a " tearing " part, full of rage and even ferocity, and became popular. In a short time later his reputation had got to London, and he was engaged at Drury Lane by Garrick, who cheerfully offered his stage even to such brethren as were likely to shine in his own line of character.

Here his powers excited admiration and ridicule. He was certainly what is called " a fine actor," conscientious, well studied, full of the character and profession, with an overweening sense of his own dignity and abilities, which yet could not be styled vanity. He had a splendid eye and a good figure, and in parts where fierce rage and blatant power were required, was excellent. But the critics soon began to find amusement in his regulated attitudes and stage " drill," to which he devoted unwearied pains, while his favourite position, known as the "handle and spout," one arm extended, the other bent and resting on his hip, was unsparingly ridiculed. Churchill gives this admirable picture of him:—

> "Mossop, attached to military plan,
> Still kept his eye fixed on his right-hand man.
> Whilst the mouth measures words with cunning skill,
> The right hand labours and the left lies still.
> With studied impropriety of speech
> He soars beyond the hackneyed critic's reach,
> *To epithets allots emphatic state,*
> *Whilst principals, ungraced, like lackeys wait.*
> In monosyllables his thunders roll,
> He, she, it, and we, ye, they, fright the soul."*

He was unsparing of his labours, and one of his characters was found written over with the most extraordinary elocutionary directions, such as "a tone, *with feeling, but low;*" "*Vast throbs of feeling;*" and the words "new device" are to be illustrated by "*face full to audience. Side look. Cunning, fretful, and musing. Smiling inward.*"

Enemies of Garrick, however, suggested to him that he was put in the background, that the manager was jealous of his talents, and purposely kept him out of the "lover" characters. His haughty, sensitive soul instantly saw a design, complete and insidious. Wretched scribes in the Press inflamed him by urging the same accusation. All the time he was figuring in Richards,

* This admirable sketch appeals to the ear as well as to the eye, and we can almost hear the stiff, rugged actor dwelling slowly on each pronoun.

Zangas, and other important parts. But he pressed for the lovers; the manager good-humouredly allowed him to make the experiment, which, as may be conceived, was a ludicrous failure, and which was naturally set down by the injured player to any cause but his own deficiencies.

"Mr. Mossop's departure," says his champion, Williams, " was partly occasioned by an affront he took from Mr. Garrick's appointing Mr. Mossop to act Richard, as we will suppose this night—and his first and best character, which stood well against Mr. Garrick's, though not so artfully and finely discriminated—and at the same time the manager secured a command from the Prince of Wales for the night following; so that when Mr. Mossop had finished Richard with remarkable credit in February 1759, to his astonishment the Mr. Palmer of that age stepped forward and said, 'To-morrow night, by command of his Royal Highness the Prince of Wales (his present Majesty), King Richard III.—King Richard by Mr. Garrick.' It gave a great damp to what Mr. Mossop had just finished; it certainly was galling, and proved duplicity and ill-nature, as well as envy."

In disgust he quitted the theatre, and in 1761 went to Dublin, where he determined to have a theatre of his own, where he could play lovers and such characters as he pleased.

This opens a chapter in Irish stage history—the struggle of Barry and Woodward against Mossop at Smock Alley Theatre, a battle that divided the city into parties, and was fought out to the ruin of all the combatants. Two prodigal managers—Barry and Woodward—were reigning in partnership at Dublin, and fancied that the whole field was secure for themselves. "The consternation," writes Tate Wilkinson, "at the news was extreme. Mr. Barry was then as passionate an inamorata as ever youthful poet fancied when he loved, and would have thrown immediate bars to the engagement with Mrs. Abington, had not a sudden and important matter of astonishment at that time started up to the amazement of every faculty of eyes, ears, &c.; for Barry and Woodward, lulled in their long wished-for security, became the dupes of their own arts, and made the wandering prodigal (Woodward) begin seriously to reflect, and severely repent his foolish conduct in leaving his enviable situation in London, and above all the horror of losing what he had saved with so much care. This dreadful alarm was no less than the certainty of a report being confirmed as real, which at first they treated as unlikely, vague, and impossible; but it proved strictly true, that Mr. Mossop, from the encouragement and instigation of all his friends, and patronised by the Countess of Brandon, of powerful sway, with many leaders of fashion, had certainly taken Smock Alley Theatre on a long lease, purposing many expensive and gaudy alterations, &c., to oppose Crow Street, in the month of October the ensuing season. Barry and Woodward (to prevent, if possible, this dreadful undertaking) made him liberal offers; nay, even humbled themselves before him, to entreat Mossop to name his own terms. All this only increased his pride, and he spurned at every kindness or emolument submitted to his acceptance and consideration. They even offered him one thousand pounds in English, and two benefits whenever he chose to take them; but all would not do, though they certainly would have been losers by his acceptance: but their situation was desperate; therefore all they could do was right, if by any means they could have effectually prevented such an opposition. Mossop's pride and obstinacy were, however, bent on monarchy, and so he was the cause of mutual ruin; but he at last suffered in a peculiar degree of punishment.

"He had saved a decent fortune, and by the absence of Barry, could have commanded a first station in London at either theatre, whenever he pleased or wished a change from Dublin; but his pride was predominant over reason, so he prostrated fame, fortune, health, and peace of mind headlong at the shrine of vanity, where sycophants hailed him with songs of triumph in full chorus, but his festal days were few and not to be envied."

A history of the Dublin stage would be a piquant contribution to dramatic annals. Mossop insolently declared that there should be but one theatre in Ireland and that he should be the sole manager. No expense was spared. Each side had their patronesses, Mossop's being the Countess of Brandon, Miss Caulfield, sister to the Earl of Charlemont, and Lady Rachael Macdonald. He was a gentleman by birth and had aristocratic sympathies; but he was above all sense of pecuniary difficulty, being absorbed in the lofty sense of his own talent. Now he could appear as a lover. The pretty English opera of 'The Maid of the Mill' was put in rehearsal, with good singers: though the performers were a little puzzled as to who was to play the tenor. Near the day of performance, however, it was announced "the part of Lord

Aimwell (*without the songs!*) by Mr. Mossop." Tate Wilkinson then gives this lively sketch of the state of things which presently followed:—

"This governor of restless players (Mossop) was not by any means blessed with a tithe of Mr. Barry's pleasing abilities as an actor, or generous qualities as a man or manager. Mr. Barry had certainly a most enchanting fascination beyond the general lot of mankind: as a proof, it was seldom either creditor or enemy left Barry in an ill-humour, however in other respects dissatisfied or disappointed. Mr. Mossop was overloaded with a quantity of combustibles, consisting of pride, insolence, arrogance, and gall.

"Early in March 1762, both the tragedy candidates, Barry and Mossop, had fixed on performing Othello on the same Monday, for their benefit play. Mossop relying on his novelty, Barry on his long-established reputation, the partisans prepared for battle; bets ran high and furious, as in the present days for pugilism. Mossop's holder of the stakes was the Countess of Brandon, heavy in demeanour, but alert in apprehension. Her ladyship solicited his Grace the Duke of Northumberland to command Mossop's night, to which he generously assented; but wisely contrived to occasion a cessation of hostilities between the two combatants, by promising to Barry, that, provided he would postpone his night to the Tuesday, he would also command that evening's entertainment, by which means the town would be kept in good-humour, the particular friends of each rest satisfied, and, his Grace also added, he should (by such attention and compliance from Mr Barry) not be deprived of the pleasure of seeing him in his favourite character of Othello, which always afforded him the highest satisfaction. Barry of course complied, and was not inwardly displeased that the critics (without a division) would have such an immediate opportunity to compare notes on the skill and superiority of the declared opponents. On this remarkable occasion each house was equally thronged, though Barry's, on the Tuesday, was the greatest receipt, as Crow Street was capable of containing more than Smock Alley; otherwise party zeal, added to curiosity, raised auditors in such superabundance as would have filled Drury Lane and Covent Garden Theatres. As to victory, Barry's Othello was so meritorious as to make Mossop's viewed at a distance only; he was as much superior in the valiant Moor as Mossop would have been to Barry in Richard or Zanga.

I sat, the evening of Mossop's benefit, in an upper box, where a lady who sat next me exclaimed on Mossop's first appearance, with an archness and humour peculiar to that nation, 'O! faith, Mossop has got two eyes in his chest?' This shrewd remark was occasioned by his wearing a heavy embossed shape (fit for Brutus or Cato), a dragon's face on the breast, with two large glaring red stones for the eyes; his face and wig being black, conveyed exactly what the lady had so ironically expressed. Mr. Barry, though masterly that night of controversy, had frequently shown himself to more advantage, merely owing to his then taking too great pains in his favourite and much esteemed part; which proves, that lucky accidents fortunately combined with nature will perchance strike out more beauties for an artist than all the most determined force of premeditation.

"Mr. Mossop that year had an Italian opera company, which was of infinite service to him, but astonishingly hurt his own consequence: for, what with parties and other diversions of routs, assemblies, concerts, &c. with which Dublin in the winter abounds, and opposed by the forces of Woodward and Barry (for they still maintained their fashion and good report), the great box nights were chiefly confined to those of the burlettas. That agreeable singer and actress *Signora De Amici* was the principal, and was almost adored; she after that greatly succeeded at the opera house in London, as the first serious woman singer. These Italian comic operas were all the rage, and were supported at the following prices: —boxes, pit, and lettices, 5s. 5d.; middle gallery, 2s. 2d.; upper gallery, 1s. 1d. Dublin was then torn to pieces by the perpetual application for one theatre or the other; it was reduced quite to a party matter. The Countess of Brandon would not be seen at Crow Street upon any account, but attended constantly at her dear Mossop's. Barry, I believe, had at least converted the ladies two to one in his favour. Barry's making love, when on the stage, left tender impressions; but yet this play-begging at last grew troublesome, and ended with fatal circumstances, of which an exact account has before been given.

"Mossop, when he had a good house, instead of endeavouring to extricate himself in any degree from his multiplicity of difficulties, grew desperate, and instead of paying either his tradesman or performers, flew to the gay circles, where he was gladly admitted; and in order to mend his broken fortune by the chance of a die or the turn up of a card—of which I believe he was ignorant, and unacquainted with the necessary arts to succeed —he has often left the theatre with a hundred guineas in his pocket, and returned home with an aching head and heart; but his guineas, with debts of honour, were all left behind. The Countess of Brandon served him greatly, it is true; but often the money she occasioned being paid at the theatre returned to her own coffers. This was the universal opinion of Dublin, and is all I can allege in that case as to its authenticity; and, as to Mossop's poverty, there needs no evidence for that unfortunate reality. This conduct, and a train of evils attendant thereon, soon preyed upon his health, involved his talents with himself, and gave bitter sours to that temper which was, in its natural source, far from being one of the best. An instance of the poverty his performers were reduced to in 1764 I will, with permission, relate.

"The 'Distressed Mother' was to be acted—Orestes Mr. Mossop; Andromache by Mrs. Burden (whom I have so often mentioned). The salaries had not been paid for several weeks, and she was in true character as the distressed *woman*. With infinite difficulty she forced access to the general—Mossop;

for it was hard to accomplish admittance on account of many inconvenient reasons, unless on a Sunday, and on that grand levée day performers and tradesmen were too menial to be admitted. But with the force of a heroine, who dauntless surmounts all barriers and tyrants at will, so Mrs. Burden burst into the 'inmost recess of his prison house,' and when arrived at the royal hall, she was as determined to preserve character; for at the awful voice of Mossop she, Andromache-like, was prostrate at the feet of her royal master, and uttered forth in tragic tones, 'O! sir, for God's sake assist me, I have not bread to eat. I am actually starving, and shall be turned out into the streets.'

"*Mossop*. (*In state.*) Wo-man!—you have five pounds per week, wo-man!

"*Mrs. Burden*. True, sir: but I have been in Dublin six months, and in all that time have only received six pounds. I call every Saturday at the office for my salary—but no money, is the answer: besides, sir, your credit and your honour are at stake; how can I play Andromache, the Trojan Queen, without black satin shoes?

"*Mossop*. Woman, begone! I insist on your having black satin shoes for Androm-a-che. And, wo-man, if you *dare* ask me for money again, I will forfeit you ten pounds, wo-man.—So ended that real tragical scene of penury and pomposity."

There were endless stories rife in the city of his straits and difficulties, the most ludicrous of which was that of the actor who, supporting him in his (histrionic) agonies, threatened to let him fall unless he promised that his salary should be paid. As Mossop hesitated, the actor, grown desperate, was about carrying out his purpose when the other consented. Difficulties and miseries of all kinds began to overwhelm him, but there can be no doubt but that the patronesses—"The Right Honourable Rooks," as one account calls them— helped to pillage him. He plunged into law proceedings with his rivals, in which he spent some £2000, and had at last to barricade himself in his house against bailiffs. All this time, as may be seen from a letter in the Garrick Correspondence, he was indebted to his old enemy for money and many friendly acts of assistance, which he acknowledges. But the struggle could not be sustained; the town at last grew tired, declaring that no one cared "a toss up, whether Mossop kicked Barry, or Barry kicked Mossop," and at last, bankrupt in fortune, and to some extent in reputation, he fled from the scene of so much disaster.

After this came a speedy and mysterious descent. He found his way to London, where, humiliated, scornful, and prouder than ever, he disdained to ask an engagement from Garrick. The latter, whose theatre was well provided, was perhaps not very eager to secure so disagreeable and difficult an auxiliary, and not unnaturally, and in the absence of a formal application, affected not to know that Mr Mossop desired to be engaged. Here was ground for a grievance, and though sensible friends begged of him to be rational and submit, he discovered that this was the old envy revived, and that Roscius was meanly jealous and afraid. It must and should come from him. Garrick of course, when the matter was made a point of submission on his side, declined to move. Some low parasites that were about Mossop inflamed the brooding actor's rage : and one more clever than the rest, David Williams, published an offensive pamphlet asking "why Mr. Mossop was not engaged," and grossly taunting Garrick with his failing powers, the feebleness of his limbs, and his lack-lustre eye.

But there was a greater change noticed in his haughty enemy. He was seen moping in lowly places, emaciated, shrunk away to half his former size—his voice grown hoarse and almost inarticulate—and half starved. It was known indeed that he had no money and was well-nigh destitute. But when friendly voices asked how his health was, the proud tragedian answered " that he never was better :" and when friendly hands offered relief, he replied haughtily that he wanted nothing.

At last, in the year 1773, the following letter from a clergyman reached Mr. Garrick. It brought news of the wretched finale.

"I found him," wrote the gentleman, " preparing for death *with that extraordinary solemnity* which accompanied all his important actions. He had gone though the general forms of the church ; but I believe only as religious and edifying forms, and unattended with any discourse on the state of his mind. His conversations with me were the most interesting that can well be conceived, and from the extreme dejection of my own mind, and the high and tragical tone in which he expressed himself, they made a dreadful impression on me. His religion was tinctured by the characters he had studied, and many of the attributes of God were the qualities of a Zanga or a Bajazet. Among other things which gave him uneasiness, and made him greatly apprehend the displeasure of that God before whom he was going to appear, his behaviour to you was not the least distressing. He accused himself severely of having attributed motives of conduct to you which he firmly believed you to be incapable of. He saw that he had been deceived by an excessive pride; and lamented the injustice he had done you not only in some pecuniary articles, but in giving ill impressions of your character to his acquaintance. The very night in which he died he renewed this conversation. He often cried out, 'O my dear friend! how mean and little does Mr. Garrick's present behaviour make me appear in your eyes, to whom I have given so different an idea of him! Great God, forgive me! Witness, my dear William, that I die not only in charity with him, but that I honour him as a great and virtuous man. God Almighty bless and prosper him for ever!"

Garrick wrote back:—"I thank you for your most affecting letter. Your account of poor Mossop's death distressed me greatly I have been often told that his friends never spoke kindly of me, and I am now at a loss what behaviour of mine, from the first moment I knew him till the time of his death, could have given him that unkind and, I hope, unmerited turn of mind against me. Had I known his distress, I should most certainly have relieved it, he was too great a credit to our profession not to have done all in our power to have made him easy if not happy."

This was the end of the ill-fated player, who expired in a mean lodging at Chelsea. Fourpence was all the money found, and the disgrace of a funeral at the expense of the parish seemed imminent. Mr. Garrick wished to save the remains of his old comrade from such an indignity; but a man of fashion, and Bencher of one of the Inns of Court, interposed. This gentleman, who had taken no notice of his unhappy nephew in his misery, now felt that the respectability of the family was in question, and defrayed the expenses of a moderate funeral.

Such is the story of the unfortunate tragedian— the proud "*high breathing Mr. Mossop*"—as Tate Wilkinson happily describes him. It makes what is perhaps the most touching episode in the annals of the stage.

CHAPTER II.

LOVE AND DEATH UPON THE STAGE.

THE instances of the elevation of actresses from the stage to be peeresses and ladies of title, are pretty well known, and have added to the dignity of the stage. Beyond the fact of the marriages themselves, which were in the nature of a surprise, there was not much romance involved, and indeed some of these episodes, such as that of Miss Farren, ended in prosy fashion by separation or divorce. The Duchesses of Bolton and St. Albans, the Countesses of Derby, Essex, Brunton, Harrington, Lady Becher, make up the brilliant histrionic roll. To this category, too, belongs the well-known story of O'Brien, the handsome actor, with Lord Ilchester's daughter, Lady Sara Strangways, which has been told and retold. For the present, therefore, this ground need not be gone over again.

But there are some episodes of less pretensoins, though of more exciting character; stories of pas-

sionate love and death—more bound up with the
stage and more fruitful of interest.

I.

THE HANDSOME CONWAY.

In the year 1810 the Dublin stage sustained
the loss of a graceful actor named Holman, and
then arrived, to supply his place, a young tragedian named William Augustus Conway, who was
six feet two inches high, and reputed, as well he
might be, the tallest actor on the stage. It was
a phenomenon to see this giant play Hamlet, and
such characters, but he gradually made his way
and became exceedingly popular. He was born in
1789, and had been sent out to Barbadoes, but had
returned when eighteen years old, and had gone on
the stage. For some years he held this high position until his reputation was made, and he attracted
the managers of Covent Garden. He was engaged
there in 1813, as second to Kemble, beside whom
he could make little impression, and soon sank
into obscurity. Presently came Miss O'Neill, and
the tall tragedian was selected as *jeune premier*,
or "lover," to play with her in all the pieces with
which she was captivating the town. This con-

trust, however, did not add to his reputation, and the critics were fond of discovering deficiencies in the *ensemble*, which they maintained might be supplied by an actor more suited to her talents and style than Mr. Conway. Even with this chance offered, which would have inspired an actor of less capability than Mr. Conway, he could make no advance. The reason was no doubt that failing which often so mysteriously hinders the progress of an otherwise good actor or actress—an inability to excite the sympathy of the audience, whom indeed they rouse in quite an opposite direction. At this moment there are artists on the stage, capable, laborious, cultivated, who with every exertion can excite only what Lamb calls "imperfect sympathy," which is but one remove from antipathy. A player infinitely their inferior utters some small phrase in a true and tender modulation, and the whole house appreciates. The cause is no doubt a certain over-consciousness and innate affectation, such as makes bashful people hard and forward. Mr. Conway was besides a good-looking actor, and was supposed to be followed by a crowd of female admirers. This too always helps to raise a barrier between the player and his audiance: the former, flattered by "the trunkful of letters" which the handsome actor always is ready to boast of, indemnifies himself by this feminine admiration for neglect upon the stage. The next step is to disdain the applause which he cannot procure, and a certain conceit and affected superiority.

Some feeling of this sort was no doubt the cause of Mr. Conway's failure. Off the stage, he received homage enough to turn his head: while the ladies at least admired him in gallant parts, such as Falconbridge and Romeo. Donaldson the actor, however, declares that, apart from physical attractions, he was excellent in these characters. The story went that "a duke's daughter" had nearly lost her wits through the fascination of this captivating player.*

Miss O'Neil, however, passed away; and presently came the great Kean, and the handsome William Augustus Conway was quite extinguished. The truth was he was stung by the perpetual ridicule and banter showered on him by the Press, especially by the personalities of 'The Mirror,'

* This is recorded in a characteristic sentence in the 'Recollections of an Actor' (Walter Donaldson). "His power over the female heart is well known: and *what it must have been may be surmised* when the daughter of a duke went about raving mad for this Apollo of an actor."

which had selected him and Elliston as special butts. This journal, which was directed by the eccentric Hill, pronounced that he had a "bad voice, which was elevated into a monotonous roar, and descended to a whisper;" that his countenance during the whole performance offered one unvaried gloomy frown, that recalled "Huntley" in a circus melodrama. These criticisms grew more and more offensive. "Mr. Conway," it was stated, "must always be tracing a circle with one leg while the other acts the part of a pivot: when he stoops to lift the child, he stretches his limbs *with the air of a lusus naturæ engaged for exhibition,* and clasps his hands to the measure of one—two—three, and a hop." This style of criticism, steadily pursued through a course of years, at last drove him from the London stage to the provincial theatres.

Coming to Bath, he was destined to find himself the hero of a grotesque adventure which offered a curious contrast to his previous *bonnes fortunes.*

There a supremely foolish old lady—who was some seventy-three years old—fell violently in love with him, and at the close of her days capped all the follies of her life. This was the famous Mrs. Piozzi, *née* Salusbury, late widow of Thrale, and still later the infatuated adorer and wife of a singer and singing master. Mr. Hayward, in his entertaining memoirs of this lady, has seriously attempted to vindicate her character; yet the fact remains that during the lifetime of her first husband, she was a light, frivolous creature, though lively enough: that she broke with the truest and noblest of characters, Johnson, because he remonstrated too warmly with her, for what seemed to him an unbecoming marriage; and that she vindicated his opinion of her judgment and conduct by offering marriage, when seventy-three years old, to an actor who might have been her grandson! This well-born lady of old ancestry and good estate, who first selected a brewer, then a singer, and finally a third-rate actor—the two latter for their personal charms—and who, at the same time, had experiences of the best society in London, where she might have found the superior attractions of wit and refinement, must have had singular tastes. The tendency of the mind that is cultivated, is to rise and not to sink.

Infatuation is indeed the name for this new passion, if we may judge by the letters of one whom it is scarcely irreverence to call a very silly old lady. They are indeed a testimony to the sagacity of Samuel Johnson, now long in his grave, and whose unsparing severity on the eve of her second marriage they more than justify. She was not old enough to have this set to the account of age; for during many years she was to be accounted the most amazingly intelligent and vivacious old lady ever known. This pitiable story adds yet another instance of that compromising delusion, to which the most eminent seem to be the victims.*

In the month of September 1819 she thus commences her amatory strains :—

"Three Sundays have now elapsed since James brought me dearest Mr. Conway's promise to write to me the very next, and were it not for the newspaper which came on Tuesday the 24th August—sending me to rest comfortable, though sick enough, and under the influence of laudanum—I should relapse into my former state of agonizing apprehension on your account; but that little darling autograph round the paper was written so steady, and so completely in the old way, whenever I look at it my spirits revive, and hope (true

---

* Of the genuineness of the following extracts there can be no question. Their authenticity is proved in a manner quite convincing; but their style is even a better proof. The letters were found at New York.

pulse of life) ceases to intermit, for a while at least, and bids me be assured we shall soon meet again. I really was very ill three or four days; but the jury of matrons who sat on my complaint acquitted the apricots which I accused, and said they (all but two) proved an *alibi*. Some of the servants, who were ill too, found out that we had, in Bessy's absence, got some mildewed tea that lay in a damp closet at the last lodging. We are now removed to a palace, a Weston palazzino, where we propose receiving Mr. Conway."

She could be very graphic and amusing, this old lady; and one of the most curious features in her letters is a sort of badinage, assumed with great art, when she found herself growing too ardent, and which seemed to plead delicately that she was privileged, and only half in earnest. That stroke of the "jury of matrons" is comic; and she rather indiscreetly alludes to "a superannuated beauty fifteen or twenty years younger than myself, but sick and dropsical; her legs hanging over her shoes." This, too, is artfully put, as who should say, " Good care and preservation do not depend on age; for here is a professed beauty far younger, and not nearly so well preserved."

The young actor, however, flagged occasionally in his devotion; was often ill, and did not write; and she would appeal to him pathetically:—

"I feel much more immediately and sincerely interested in our own meeting after such cruel illness and dangers, and a silence that has shaken my courage more than all the savage shoutings of this new-fangled reformation. Good-night; and God bless my valued friend, for whose perfect recovery and long-continued happiness I will pray till the post comes in. Yes; and till life goes *out* from poor H. L. P. I would keep up my spirits —as you wish me—and your spirits too. But how can I? Send a newspaper at least. O, for a breath of intelligence, however short, respecting health and engagements!"

She did not, however, omit appeals of a substantial shape:—

"I wrote to fine Mr. Davie Robinson, Villiers Street, in the Strand, and bade him, when he sent my stock of wine to Bath, put half-a-dozen bottles of the very same in a basket and deliver to Mrs. Rudd, 41 Gerrard Street, Soho."

The basket unfortunately miscarried. Still "I wish my beloved friend to keep his spirits up, but have enough to do on his dear account to keep up my own. Yet shall not the one alleviating drop of comfort, as you kindly call my letters, ever fail. Mrs. Stratton saw the horrid paragraph inserted in the *Courier*—she writes with all possible tenderness, and, I really do believe, true concern. Mr. Bunn's elegant expressions of friendship pleased me too." Elegant expressions of friendship! Here we enter on the sentimental strain; and indeed love-making or love-writing, at this epoch, seems to have followed the model of Yorick and Eliza:

"Here am I, however, praying most fervently for your restoration to all that makes life desirable, and giving God thanks for the power He lends me of affording solace to the finest soul, the fairest emanation of its celestial origin that ever was enclosed in human clay. Such clay! But we must all be contented to bear our cross. The paschal lamb—type of our blessed Saviour—was ordered to be eaten," &c.

This, too, is another expedient with elderly lovers—to blend religion with their affection; and as we have seen, the artful Yorick become paternal and highly clerical in his exhortations, but Mrs. Piozzi verges on the profane. As

Christmas draws on she touches a congenial string:

"Accept, dearest Mr. Conway, *of a real Christmas pie*: it will be such a nice thing for you when, coming late home, there is no time for a better supper; but Bessy begs you will not try to eat the crust; it will keep for weeks this weather. The fleece should be a golden one, had I the magic powers of Medea; but I do think I was baby enough to be ashamed last night of owning I had not three pounds in the house, except your money, laid by for my benefit-ticket, which shall be replaced before that day comes."

But he got to Bath at last, and the following agitated letter must have made the invalid smile:

"Half-dead Bessy—more concerned at what I feel for you than what she feels for herself—brings this note. Mrs. Pennington left me in real affliction; and if she found no billet at the Elephant and Castle directed to her from Kingsmead, will carry home a half-broken heart. Let my maid see you, for mercy's sake. 'Lord, ma'am,' said she, 'why if Mr. Conway was at Birmingham, you would send me; and now he is only three streets off.' (Artful maid! Here also following the immemorial precedents; aged spinsters and widows, from Mrs. Wadman downwards, always accepting such comfort from their familiars.) " Go I WILL," adds Mrs. Piozzi, in large capitals; " if I die upon the road, rather than see you swallowing down agony, and saying nothing but how well you are to everybody, when I know you are wretched beyond telling!" Instead of Bessy, James goes; and Mr. Conway was implored to let him at " least see and speak to you." Motives of delicacy would of course account for the substitution.

Here, in another letter, it seems as if Mr. Sterne himself was beginning :—

"I would not hurry you for the world. Take your own time, and do it your own way; or rather suffer nature to do it—that has done so much for you; more, I do think, than for any mortal man. See what a scar the surgeon, however skilful, would have made in that beautiful neck; while nature's preparation, through previous agony, made suppurating ease come on unfelt; and the wound heals almost without a cicatrix, does it not? So will it be with the mind. My own hasty folly and my ' violent love outran the pauser Reason.' Whilst I am advising my beloved patient, however, to turn the torrent of his fancy toward the past occurrences of human life, the dear pathetic letter now in my bosom forced me on the same method this forenoon, when my heart really sunk at the thought of such coarse conduct."

This high-flown style is delicious; and *suppurating ease*" is true medical sentiment. Mr. Conway had been contemned by a young lady to whom he had paid attention, on the ground of his inferior station and birth. His patroness and admirer is furious, and refurbishes some of those old weapons with which she had defended her Piozzi. His family was superior to hers, '*des deux côtés, je sais ce que je dis.*' She went to a party, and the image of the Adonis thus attends her :—

" Who, I wonder, was that tall man I met at my last party? his aspect shocked and haunted me like a spectre, so apparently majestic in misfortune. The master of the house was pointing me out to him, as if to win his attention; but no look, no smile ensued. He was not like you, except his lofty carriage. Yet I kept on thinking, so will my Conway stand when next I see him. It was an odd feel; and your distress presented itself so forcibly to my imagination at the moment, that my mind instinctively understood—all was indeed over."

All this is incoherent and strange. Again the maid comes on the scene: "Bessy cries; but begs me not to lose my life between my scorn of your tormentors, and tenderness for your health."

But it is not uncharitable to suppose that Bessy was looking for a substantial legacy. The old lady was presently suffering all the torments of jealousy; and certainly it is pitiable, if not laughable, to see the condition of the poor dame descending even to the meanness of depreciating a rival.

Mrs. Piozzi writes with delight how she treated this family, who had dared to trifle with her Conway. It was probably the old story—a young girl flattered at the attentions of a handsome young fellow unsuitable in station, and the object of her civility interpreting it as serious encouragement.

"Now, however, I rise to say how the evening at Eckersall's passed off. Mrs. Stratton and her eldest granddaughter came early; so I returned their salutation much as usual—only refusing the hands I could not touch—and talked with Mr. Fuller about ancient Thebes, its hundred gates, &c. The young lady's airy manner—such as you describe rightly, contrasting with your own cruel situation—quite shocked me. No crying, no castdown looks, no whimpering, as last year—changeful as the weather or the wind, she seems at perfect ease. Mrs. Stratton not so. Waddling up to me in the course of the night, she said she wanted to talk with me. 'Impossible!' was the reply. 'My life is spent in such a crowd of late.'—'But on a particular subject, Mrs. Piozzi.'—'Lord, ma'am, who can talk on particular subjects in an assembly-room? and the King ill beside!' So there it ended; and for me there it shall end."

Mr. Conway could not have been in the least obliged to her for this championship. No doubt he would have been eager to know what Mrs. Stratton had to say. Her being "quite shocked" at the young lady's airy manner is true old woman's spite. But presently she cannot contain her spite and jealousy:—

"'Tis not a year and a quarter since dear Conway, accepting of my portrait sent to Birmingham, said to the bringer, 'O, if your lady but retains her friendship—O, if I can but keep her patronage—I care not for the rest.' And now, when that friendship follows you through sickness and through sorrow—now that her patronage is daily rising in importance — upon a lock of hair given or refused by *une petite traîtresse* hangs all the happiness of my once high-spirited and high-blooded friend. Let it not be so. **EXALT THY LOVE, DEJECTED HEART,** and rise superior to such narrow minds. Do not, however, fancy she will ever be punished in the way you mention: no, no; she'll wither on the thorny stem, dropping the faded and ungathered leaves; a china rose, of no good scent or flavour, false in apparent sweetness, deceitful when depended on — unlike the flower produced in colder climates, which is sought for in old age, preserved *even after death* a lasting and an elegant perfume—a medicine too, for those whose shattered nerves require *astringent remedies!*"

Then she entered on a religious homily. It was preaching, she owned, but still it came from "a heart, as Mrs. Lee says, twenty-six years old, and, as H. L. P. feels it to be, all your own." She would "die to serve him;" and sends a bottle of wine, also a partridge. "The Courtenays all inquired for my Conway; all who seek favour of me ask for you; all but —." Which aposiopesis, of course, is for the benefit of the little *traîtresse*. Her indefatigable arts in trying to propitiate him show ingenuity. She, as it were, flies up and down, driving a nail here, a nail there, into the coffin of his affection for her rival. Yet it is easy to see her uneasiness, as the ungrateful thought must have flashed across her at times, that she was *too old* for these dalliances. Her impulse then was to stifle any such association in his mind by the judicious offering of wine, of a partridge, or, more frequently still, by taking and disposing of *tickets* for his benefit. The mixture of flattery—the wish to make herself of importance, and, at the same time give *him* the idea that his merits alone were the cause of the sale of the tickets—this little contention of motives can be read plainly in the following: " I was happy to see my dear friend's handwriting, as soon as I came home, and the tickets. I must certainly have another box secured in my name, if you have no objection. You see by the inclosed how they will insist on coming to what they call my places. My Welsh friends, however, have more wit. Mr. and Mrs. Lutwyche gave me two bank-notes for two tickets, and they must have front seats in the next *loge* to where I sit myself."

It would almost seem that he was disappointed at her so cavalierly refusing to listen to what the mother of his beloved had to say, for the conversation came off later. Some of the passages are worth noting as touches of human character.

This was at the end of February 1820, and this is the last of these curious letters.

It was rumoured in Flintshire, Mr. Hayward says, that she proposed marriage to him, and that she offered Sir T. Salusbury a large sum for the family seat in Wales, which she wished to settle on the actor. This Mr. Hayward dismisses as a mere rumour, not worthy of any serious consideration. It is admitted however, that Conway showed the late Mr. Mathews a letter from Mrs. Piozzi, offering marriage.* But such proof is hardly needed—any one who follows the details of her infatuation for Conway, will see that her inflammable nature could not resist the passion which had taken possession of her.

Within a month of her last letter, in May 1821, this strange old lady died, aged eighty-two years. The young actor pursued his stage career. It is not mentioned whether he " took," as the phrase runs, anything under her will. He certainly might have had reasonable expectations, even as compensation for the ridicule he must have endured in Bath circles. He pursued his theatrical course,

* See the 'New Monthly Magazine,' April 1861.

but seems to have failed everywhere, or to have left an impression of what was neither satisfaction nor dissatisfaction, and which is about as bad as failure. Disgusted at this indifference, he went to America, and completed his series of failures out there. Too sensitive to laugh at newspaper squibs and critiques, or even to learn the art of appearing indifferent, he sank into despondency, and became "serious." This again developed into a morbid dejection. On a voyage from New York to Charleston it was noticed how silent and dejected he was, and how, though the weather was raw, he persisted in wearing only the lightest summer apparel. On the 24th of January, 1828, when the passengers were going down to dinner, he told the captain "he should never want dinner more," and presently flung himself overboard. The body was never recovered. His effects were sold, and among them were the curious letters which may have excited the amusement and pity of the reader.*

* They are published in a little pamphlet by Mr. J. Russell Smith, of Soho.

II.

LA BELLE MISS HENRIETTE.

In the year 1818, a tall handsome girl, announced as Miss Smithson, made her appearance in London, and was received with some favour. Her talents were considered not very striking, but she had a correct style, and showed evidences of study. She was indeed no more than a third-rate actress, and her name is now scarcely familiar to any but the professed students of stage chronicles. She came from Ireland, where she had been carefully educated under the patronage of ladies of rank who took an interest in her. If the stage as a profession has been disparaged it is certainly the fault of its members; for society, even of the highest and most refined order, has always been ready to open its ranks to actresses who have made a reputation for *genuine* acting. There is even an anxiety to cultivate the acquaintance of legitimate performers, and a long list, from Mrs. Siddons at the beginning of the century, to Mrs. Scott Siddons in our day, could be made out in support of this statement. It is only when the stage is perverted to purposes of *exhibition*, as in the case of burlesque pieces of a vulgar order, that an exclusion is deservedly maintained. Miss Smithson soon, as the stage chronicles are careful to tell us, found a friendly patroness in Lady Castlecoote; and further, whenever she had a benefit "the names of Mrs. Coutts, Lady and Sir Charles Doyle, and the Countess of Belmore regularly appeared in her books." Miss Smithson, therefore, might have perhaps been recollected as a correct, well-trained, interesting actress, esteemed by her audiences, as well as by a circle of distinguished friends and patrons. Most of these would have been surprised to hear that she was destined to be the heroine of a French melodramatic romance.

In the summer of the year 1827, Laurent, an old clerk of the Galignanis, who had turned manager, and, from long training in the well-known library at the Rue Vivienne, had acquired a good knowledge of English and English manners, conceived the idea of bringing an English company to Paris. He was liberal in his offers, and determined to engage only good artists. He secured Abbott, a pleasant comedian, as stage manager and actor; Liston, Charles Kemble, and Miss Smithson; with some others. He offered twenty-four napoleons a week to the leading performers, and paid the expenses to and from Paris of the whole party.

There happened to be a gentle fit of Anglomania abroad, one of those attacks which agitate the emotional French: and this was in favour of the English company. Otherwise it may be said, without contradiction, that the English drama is on the whole unintelligible to the French. Of the better-known Shakespere plays, such as 'Othello' and 'Hamlet,' the story is familiar, and they are able to follow a good actor with some general perception of what he is about. Rage and jealousy is recognisable in all countries and all languages. Again, this performance was on the eve of the great romantic revival, and the young man Alexander Dumas, who was to be one of its apostles, was, as he tells us in his diverting memoirs, an assiduous visitor to the Favart Hall, where the performances were given. He was enchanted with the English plays and players; and confesses, which is a good deal from a Frenchman, that they had a vast influence on his own genius.

The series opened with a performance of the 'Rivals,' in which Liston, as Acres, produced not the slightest effect. Not a smile was seen on the faces of the audience. The disgusted low-comedian, who at home could produce a roar by a single glance of his droll eye, refused to appear again, and went home denouncing the Frenchmen as "a set of jackasses." This was an inauspicious commencement. Sheridan's 'School for Scandal' was later tried, but received with perfect gravity. The most amusing incident occurred at a later period, when Macready was engaged to perform Othello. This he did with such effect, that when the curtain fell, some forty or fifty of the audience leaped upon the stage and insisted on overwhelming the tragedian with their embraces. In their enthusiasm, they forgot the artificial character of the Moor's swarthiness, and many of the gentlemen showed on their faces tokens of the honour they had enjoyed.

It was then thought that tragedy would be more effective, and Miss Smithson came forward in the agonizing character of Jane Shore. To the surprise of all at home, the chord was touched, the fair Smithson was discovered to be handsome and interesting—to have an exquisitely touching voice —to be full of fire and real tragic feeling. The Parisians began to rave of "la Smithson," or "Smeet sown," as it no doubt became in their mouths, and the piece was performed five and twenty nights. In the various French memoirs and criticisms we come on allusions to this actress, who is spoken of with praises that we should have thought suited only to the talents of an O'Neill or a Jordan. In the Drury Lane green-room, where she had held rank as a decent "walking lady," there was much wonder at this success. In Paris, the Royal Family used to attend, and the Duke of Berry, who had picked up some English in exile, and could use English hunting oaths with good effect, was often found behind the scenes. But it was not in this august circle that her chief admirer was to be found.

A young medical student of ardent spirit, with a passionate love for music, chanced to witness one of her performances, and was captivated by the "belle Henriette Smithson," who had played Ophelia. This was the young Berlioz, a wild and irregular genius, whose essays are as characteristic as his music. His love became a frantic passion. Already a composer, he found himself compelled to express his ardour in symphoniac "Deaths of Ophelia," and other Shakesperean subjects. His soul was possessed by the one subject, and could not find rest. Betimes he would fly from Paris to the country, and after wandering about all day and walking miles, would hurry back in the evening to the theatre to witness the performances of his idol. His longing desire was to attract her notice: for up to this time he was but one of the indistinct atoms of an audience, and might have attended for weeks without his face ever attracting observation. In his desperation he contrived, though without money, to get up a concert for the performance of his works. But a disastrous failure was the only result, and his strange style seemed opposed to all canons of good music. Following the precedent of many an enamoured apprentice or draper's assistant, he began to address letters to the object of his adoration, but these were of so frantic and extravagant a description that Miss Smithson strictly enjoined her maid to take in no more from that source. This mortifying rebuff, as may be imagined, did not cure him. By superhuman exertions he arranged a second concert, and contrived that it should be given at the very theatre where Miss Smithson was playing. Their names actually appeared in the same bill—his for the morning, hers for the evening, performance; this did honour to the perseverance of the love sick youth. But it was only an apparent *rapprochement*. The concert succeeded, but Ophelia, it would seem, was not present, and was ignorant whether it succeeded or failed. The following morning he saw her get into her travelling carriage and set off for England. Thus did the romance appear likely to end.

Distracted at this loss, he was thinking of some desperate step, when an ingenious friend furnished the strangest remedy ever dreamed of in the vagaries of the gentle passion. This gentleman, who was a German pianist, drew his attention to a young actress of the Boulevards, who was the image of the absent Smithson. The idea was seized on by the deserted swain, who accepted this new object as a sort of image or deputy, and transferred his passion and attentions to her. The actress returned his affection. The lover presently obtained the "prize of Rome" at the Conservatoire, and had to set out for that city to pursue his studies. While there news reached him of the marriage of his deputy flame. In a new paroxysm of despair, he fell into fresh extravagance, and set off for France furnished with *three* pistols— for the husband, the faithless actress, and himself. At Genoa he took a last look at a "*Fantastic Symphony*" which he had composed, and dissolved into tears as he thought of the works of which he might be depriving the world. This produced a gentle reaction, but a sudden paroxysm caused him to fling himself into the sea, from whence he was rescued with infinite difficulty. All this might seem incredible but for the well-known and recorded extravagance of other Frenchmen under the influence of a passion which, in their country, cannot be called "the gentle" one. His letter to Victor Hugo detailing his rescue has been preserved,* and supports this account of the transaction. The "ducking," as it would be called in prose, seems to have restored him to his senses. He complains of having been "hooked like a salmon," spread for a quarter of an hour for dead in the sun, after which he had "violent vomitings for a whole hour." Calmer thoughts succeeded, and he resolved that he would live for the sake of his two sisters and for art. So he returned to Rome to finish his studies.

Two years later he was in Paris again, bringing with him the "Fantastic Symphony" which had been inspired by the enchanting Smithson. He chose his rooms exactly opposite those which *she* had occupied. He made some inquiries. Joy and rapture! she was actually in Paris, now

* 'Les Contemporains,' article "Berlioz," p. 45.

manageress of a theatre and about to resume her performances! He determined to resume his old passion—and could do so under favourable auspices. He was now an artist. He resolved to try his fortune once more—with a concert. A friend engaged to bring her, and he had the exquisite satisfaction of seeing her seated among the audience. The "Fantastic Symphony" of this fantastic being, with all its groans and cries, and ejaculations of love, rage, and despair, produced the effect. We are told that the young actress seemed to perceive that she was the source that inspired these strange sounds. She was seen to weep; and the next day graciously consented that the eccentric young composer, who wooed in so strange a fashion, should be introduced. He almost at once proposed marriage.

Some serious difficulties, however, interposed. Her parents naturally objected to an alliance which was so unsuitable in every way. So wild and almost childish a lover would be likely to prove an undesirable husband for a decorous and well brought-up English girl. She too had her troubles. The speculation she had embarked in was a foolish one. Almost the first night she learned how temporary had been her attraction:

and the fickle Frenchmen did not now care to go and look at *la belle Henriette.* The poor actress had to sink all her savings in this project—and in a short time, was compelled to withdraw from the undertaking. She became *bankrupt,* and was left without a shilling.

The young composer, however, to his credit, prosecuted his suit. The fair Henriette at last consented, and in the year 1833 they were married. But disaster seemed to pursue them: for only a few days after the ceremony she fell and broke her leg. It was found, too, that the heroine had brought him some heavy debts as her portion. But he behaved with gallantry and devotion, worked hard, gave concerts and lessons, and succeeded, by paying the creditors a little, in inducing them to wait. Meanwhile his reputation began to spread; but with that reputation came violent prejudices, which operated on his character and made him fierce and combative—ferocious in his animosities—and excited hosts of enemies. The story of his musical life is well known to musicians and literary men, and has little to do with the present episode.

It is awkward to have to tell that the result of this romantic and stormy courtship was unsatisfactory. The French writers say that the *ménage* was an unhappy one, all owing to "la belle Smithson" whom he had so loved. She did not make him happy. Possessed by the demon of Jealousy, she disturbed the peace of the household, so that living together became impossible. In other words, the impulsive husband was liable at any moment to become the victim of some new passion which his English wife did not perhaps tolerate; the hero of the three pistols, the drowning, &c., was most likely to be the disturber of the peace of the household.

But in the year 1851, when she was seized with an attack of paralysis, it is recorded that nothing could exceed the devotion and attention of her husband. The same year she died, and thus ended a very curious and little known episode connected with a romance of the stage.

III.

"LOVE AND MADNESS."

A notorious and disagreeable character that figured in the fast life of the last century was the Earl of Sandwich. His private character was of the most abandoned sort. In his public capacity he was highly unpopular; the nickname of "Jemmy Twitcher" showed in what contempt he was held. His curious "shambling" walk was always being ridiculed; even the poor old king, when his wits had gone beyond recall, was heard to repeat with a kind of imbecile chuckle the name of "Jemmy Twitcher." The most odious feature in his career was his hypocritical disloyalty to Wilkes, with whom he had shared in many an orgy, but whose indecorums he stood up to reprobate in the House of Lords—being shocked by his outrages against public morality.

About the year 1762 this exemplary character, when making some purchases in a milliner's shop close to Covent Garden, was attracted by a very handsome girl who was serving behind the counter. This was a Miss Ray, a common labourer's daughter who had found her way to London from Elstree, and had been apprenticed to a mantle maker at Clerkenwell. From a picture of her by Dance, her beauty would seem to have been a little exaggerated, and there was more an expression of interest than of beauty. This accords with her character, which was retiring and amiable. Within a short time the milliner's apprentice had left the shop, and had entered upon a regular course of accomplishments, which was pursued for some two years, at the expense of her noble patron. It was discovered that she had a fine voice, and one of "Jemmy Twitcher's" redeeming points being a passion for music, she soon began to display her talent in a remarkable fashion, and became a singer of merit.

She was now installed at Hinchinbroke, Lord Sandwich's seat, where the lady of the house had to submit, with as good a grace as she could, to what was at the time a not unfashionable species of affront. It was, however, in some sense varnished over by the prosecution of musical entertainments, oratorios, &c., in which the intruding lady took her part, and indeed made an awkward position as little offensive as possible. For many years this relation continued. Miss Ray's musical reputation increased. The noble amateur was fond of giving entertainments, to which all the persons of fashion and position were eager to be invited, and where Miss Ray always took the part of leading soprano. She received lessons from Giardini, then a singer of eminence, and also from Mr. Bates. Lord Sandwich's concerts at Hinchinbroke show indeed that amateur music was then more advanced than would at present be supposed.

The oratorio of 'Jephthah' was a favourite piece. The Duke of Manchester's military band made part of the orchestra. Mr. Bates led, while the noble host, as Mr. Cradock, a frequent guest, comically describes it, "took the kettle drums, to *animate the whole.*" The 'Non Nobis' was sung during dinner, and sometimes a glee. Miss Ray, it was admitted, was the chief attraction, and even the ladies were pleased to remark how little "she assumed" upon her situation. Lady Blake indeed was so far carried away by her interest as "to advance between the parts" (it is the fussy Mr. Cradock who tells us), and address some compliments to the fair soprano. It was noticed, however, that the retiring Miss Ray was really embarrassed at this attention. She wished for no recognition beyond a musical one, and the host was heard to remark to a friend that he wished a hint could be given to the lady of rank who had paid the attention; "for," he added, "there is a boundary line in my family which I should not wish to see exceeded. This sort of thing might upset all our pleasant music meetings." However, when the Bishop of Lincoln (Dr. Green) was also impelled to go up to compliment her on her singing of 'Brighter Scenes,' or of 'Shepherds, I have lost my love,' or when Mrs. Hinchcliffe, a bishop's lady, protested "feelingly," " I declare I am quite ashamed to sit opposite to her and take no notice, she is so modest and unassuming!" it showed that Lady Blake's indiscretion had been rather severely dealt with, and that " our pleasant music meetings " could not have been in any serious danger of being overset. A censorious public was, however, a little sarcastic on this toleration by bishops, and some indifferent verses were written on the subject :—

" When nobles and bishops and squires are so silly
To attend the levée of Miss Ray and of Billy,
When to show most respect for the lord of the place is,
By listening to fiddlers—and praising his mistress.
If this be the case, and you do not dissemble,
The cause do you ask ? To be sure it is Handel ;
There's a lord beats a drum, not yet by it disgraced,
Since a bishop, perchance, by Giardini is placed ;
So the high and the low are all jumbled together
In order that Jephthah may go off the better."

A letter of hers which has been preserved shows that the education which her protector was said to have secured for her, was not of a very high order :—

"June 27, 1774.

"Yesterday was favoured with yours, which found me very unwell indeed, but I myself sent the score of Jephthah directly to Miss Davis. It would have given me great pleasure to have heard Miss Davis; and I am very much obliged to you for all your polite attention to me. My opinion is that every person will be pleased and delighted with her. Though I cannot be present at your most respectable meeting, which I hope will be very full; you will have my best wishes; and that you may continue well yourself. Should you have any other commands pray let me know them, and they shall be readily obeyed."

Some years passed by, when Mr. Cradock—who was a sort of amateur littérateur, and assiduously strove to secure a portion of the spare moments of men like Goldsmith, Johnson, Garrick, and others—was asked to vote for a candidate professor at Cambridge, a great friend of Lord Sandwich's, and on his return was pressed to stay at Hinchinbroke. As he and his host were entering the house they met a couple of officers, who had come to call; one of whom was Major Reynolds an acquaintance of Lord Sandwich, the other a Captain of the 68th Foot, who was recruiting at Huntingdon. The Major was asked to dine, and then begged to be allowed to introduce his friend Captain Hackman,—who was also invited to stay.

They had a small party at dinner—the two officers, Lord Sandwich, Mr. Cradock, and Miss Ray, who came down attended by a lady friend. After dinner there was a rubber of whist. Captain Hackman from the first moment was quite fascinated by Miss Ray. He did not join in the game, but "requested leave to look over the cards." Lord Sandwich "retired early." The lady was indeed now titular mistress of the mansion, and, it may be presumed, had by this time driven out the rightful hostess. This little entertainment was to prove the beginning of one of the most painful tragedies of the time.

The officer had commenced life by being articled to a merchant, but soon exchanged this profession for the army. For the next three weeks after the dinner he was hanging about Hinchinbroke; he used to meet Miss Ray on her rides about the place, and being good looking believed that he had recommended himself to her good graces. He felt, however, that he had nothing to offer in exchange for her present situation; he was very poor, and his brother-in-law, Booth, was a humble tradesman in Cheapside. She was mother of a family, and had no inclination for following about a marching regiment.

In this state of affairs he obtained an introduction to the Commander-in-Chief in Ireland, and set off for that country, in the hope of obtaining some military preferment there. In this he failed, and the infatuated man, who had been a merchant's clerk and a soldier, now once more changed his profession, took orders, and became the Rev. Mr. Hackman and Curate of Wyveston in Norfolk.

This, however, did not advance his suit, though he was more pressing than ever in his attentions. Miss Ray's situation now became embarrassing. It was thought she returned the affection of her admirer, and was eager to settle down respectably. Lord Sandwich was advanced in life. The customary "settlement," the object of a prudent ambition with ladies in her situation, had not been made; and her children were not provided for. Her musical gifts, too, had so developed, that she was looking to an engagement at the opera, where an actual offer of £3000 and a free benefit had been made to her. On the other hand, she felt the weight of her obligations to one who for seventeen years had been her friend and protector. Comparing her, indeed, with other ladies of her condition, she might be considered comparatively respectable, and perhaps more a victim than a

sinner. She at last seems to have found the
almost frantic advances of the Rev. Mr. Hackman too embarrassing, and amounting to an annoyance. She was anxious to check his importunities, to be rid of so dangerous a suitor, and at last refused to see him. Meanwhile Lord Sandwich was becoming highly unpopular; offensive ballads were sung under the Admiralty windows: and in a riot which arose owing to the Keppel acquittal, she and Lord Sandwich had to escape in the night from the Admiralty, and were in much alarm from mob violence. The unfortunate woman was indeed prepared for the catastrophe that was presently to follow, by presages in the shape of alarms, jealousies, indecision, and anxiety. A friend or companion was living with her, imposed on her, it was later stated, as a sort of duenna, by Lord Sandwich.

The Rev. Mr. Hackman was in town, and living in Craven Street. He at last began to be persuaded that she had finally withdrawn her affections from him, and grew almost desperate. It was now April 17, 1779, and he had discovered that she was to go out for the evening. He tried to find out where she was going, but she refused to tell him. This filled the measure, and led him to resolve on his final purpose. He stationed himself in a coffee house at Charing Cross to watch, and saw her carriage go by into the Strand; he followed and tracked her to Covent Garden Theatre: where, with her friend Signora Galli, the singer, she occupied a conspicuous position in a front box. The opera was 'Love in a Village.'

All through the night Mr. Hackman was flitting restlessly about the house, now in the galleries, now in the lobbies, frantically watching, and now retiring to the Bedford Coffee House to drink brandy and water. He saw a great deal that must have inflamed his fury; the "three gentlemen, all connected with the Admiralty, who came and occasionally paid their compliments to them." Mr. Macnamara, an Irish Templar, had also paid his respects to the ladies, and Miss Ray had been seen to "coquet with him." The opera came to a conclusion; the lobbies filled, and the Piazza echoed with the voices of chairmen and link boys calling for coaches.

Miss Ray's carriage was waiting, and she herself was coming out. Mr. Macnamara, the Irish Templar, was at hand, and observing that she was somewhat crushed in the crowd, made his way to her and gave her his arm. The agonized clergyman had seen all her gaiety—her coquetry with the Templar, and her carelessness as to *his* absence. He had pistols in his pocket, but had certainly come out that night with no design against her. His purpose was to wait for her at the theatre door, shoot himself, and fall a bloody corpse at her feet. The spectacle of all that enjoyment, her smiles to the dashing Templar who was conducting her out, filled him with a sort of frenzy. The unfortunate lady had her foot on the step of the carriage, when a man pulled her gown; as she turned round, she felt a pistol touch her forehead. Another second and it was discharged, and the Templar saw her clap her hand to her forehead—an amazing exertion, for the skull was later found to be divided into halves by the shot. The next moment the man had fired at his own head and was stretched on the ground. The unhappy lady had sunk down bathed in her blood, with which the Templar, as he attempted to raise her, found himself covered. The scene may be imagined—at once horrible and picturesque; the flaring torches—the ladies in their dresses and ornaments—the shouts for help—the wretched victim in her finery, "Signora Galli" bending over her and no doubt in hysterics—and the murderer on the flags, frantically beating his own head with the butt end of his pistol, and shrieking "Kill me! kill me!" for the ball had only grazed the skull. "Thus," says the customary notice of the day, "terminated the existence of the beautiful, the favoured, and yet the unfortunate Miss Ray.... There was scarcely any polite art in which she was not an adept, or any part of *female literature* (?) with which she was not conversant." Her conversation offered an "unparalleled delicacy which characterised her through life. In short," goes on the obituary notice in a delicious passage, "we may pronounce Miss Ray to have been a very amiable and valuable character; *for the susceptible, even among the most chaste*, will scarce think one frailty an adequate counterpoise to so many good qualities: but, by placing that single frailty to nature and her sex, must join in the general pity for so worthy and accomplished a woman."

The body of "the lovely victim" was carried across the street to the Shakspeare Coffee House, where also the murderer was conveyed. An express was sent off to the Admiralty to Lord Sandwich, who was expecting her home to supper at half-past ten. As she did not arrive, he grew tired, and after waiting an hour, went to bed. He was roused up at midnight by his black servant, who came with the news. He was quite stupefied and overwhelmed by the shock—or as the fashionable newspapers of the day expressed it more appropriately, " his Lordship fell into the most lamentable agonies, and expressed a sorrow that did infinite honour to his feelings : *indeed, what feelings must that man have who would not be agonized at such a spectacle!*" The latter portion of the sentence, it will be seen, almost annuls the compliment in the first.

Hackman's wound was dressed, and his pockets were searched. There were found two letters, one addressed to Miss Ray, containing a last passionate appeal, and fresh protestations of his attachment—which showed that he had not made up his mind until perhaps he had reached the theatre, to take any violent step. The second letter was to his brother-in-law, Mr. Booth, in which he set out his resolution to destroy himself, and the cause. He could not live, he said, without Miss Ray. And since he saw that he was now excluded, from the house, and that she persistently refused to see him, he had determined to destroy himself. He was besides overwhelmed with debt.

He did not care to live, and wished his brother all the felicity that he himself dared not to hope for. It was inferred from these letters that he only intended to kill himself, and that he was driven by a sudden and uncontrollable fit of fury to kill her. Beauclerk, discussing this point with Johnson, urged that the two pistols were intended for himself alone—one being kept in reserve in case the first missed fire or merely wounded. The probability, indeed, is that he left his house with the intention of taking his own life; and that what he had seen at the theatre and at the end of the performance, had suddenly determined him to add the other crime to the first. This seems to have been the view of Justice Blackstone at the trial.

When Hackman was at the Shakspeare, he was asked by the Templar, the question that seems to be always rather indiscreetly put on such occasions, "Why he had done such a bloody deed?" and answered calmly that this was not the place for such questions. He then earnestly desired to see his victim, supposing that she was still alive, and being told that she was dead, begged that her poor remains might not be exposed to the view of the curious. Sir John Fielding, the blind magistrate, arrived, at five in the morning, and finding that his wounds were not serious, made out his committal to the Bridewell. He was at once carried to the prison; and when he arrived there he broke out into frantic protestations of his attachment, and talked of his victim with all the extravagance of the maddest love.

That day the news was all over the town. Parson Warner, perhaps the most disreputable member of his cloth in his day, was dining at "Harry Hoare's" with a jovial party, where all the talk was about Miss Ray. Knowing his friend George Selwyn's indecent curiosity or craze about such matters, he called at the tavern where the remains of the unfortunate lady were laid out waiting the inquest, and did his best to get in and have a view of them; so as to send a full account of the morbid spectacle. But he had no interest, he said, with the doorkeepers—and money was refused. The newspapers, later affected to joke on Mr. Selwyn's interest in these matters, and declared that he was detected sitting at the head of the corpse, disguised in a mourning cloak. On the fourteenth day she was taken down to Elstree and interred in a vault there. Her father, to whom she had always allowed a small pension, was still alive. Lord Sandwich retired to the country, and indeed altogether from society. When he emerged, however, not being able to resist his favourite music, performers would awkwardly select airs in which the deceased singer used to distinguish herself, such as 'Shepherds, I have lost my love!' and though "Mr. Bates" saw the unfortunate character of the melody, it was too late to rectify the mistake, and his Lordship was seen to retire from the party in great distress.

The trial came on. The prisoner was determined to plead guilty, but at the last moment was prevailed on, perhaps by the entreaties of his sister, to enter the usual plea. The case was of course proved conclusively. He made a rather pathetic defence. He said he had no wish to live. "I stand here the most wretched of human beings, and confess myself criminal in a high degree: yet while I acknowledge with shame and repentance that my determination against my own life was formed and complete, I protest with that regard to truth which becomes my situation that the will to destroy her who was dearer to me than life was never mine till a momentary frenzy overpowered me, and induced me to commit the deed I deplore. I have no wish to avoid the punishment which the laws of my country appoint for my crime: but being already too unhappy to feel a punishment in death or a satisfaction in life, I submit myself with penitence and patience to the disposal and judgment of Almighty God." This was of course a prepared appeal, and has rather an artificial tone. On the other hand, a person in such a situation may not be able to trust to a natural eloquence, and though the words may have been conned by rote, the sentiment might be perfectly genuine. He received sentence with calm composure and Lady Upper Ossory was able to write for the satisfaction of her friend Selwyn, who was still greedy of particulars, " that Mr. Hackman's behaviour *was glorious yesterday!*" This is good evidence of the " toadyism " with which the opulent bachelor was gratified, ladies of rank and condition being thus eager to cater for his unseemly mania.

Lord Carlisle, who specially attended the execution in order to furnish particulars to his friend Mr. Boswell, was even more fortunate, and was privileged with a seat in the mourning coach opposite the prisoner. "I am this moment returned from it," wrote the Earl. " Everybody inquired after you, you have friends everywhere. The poor man behaved with great fortitude: no appearances of fear were to be perceived, but many evident signs of contrition and repentance. He was long at his prayers, and when he flung down his handkerchief for a signal for the cart to move on, Jack Ketch, instead of instantly whipping on his horses, jumped on the other side of him to snatch up the handkerchief, lest he should lose his rights, and then returned to the head of the cart; then, with the gesture so faithfully represented by your friend Lord Wentworth, *Jehu'd him out of the world.*" It seems amazing that so indecent a tone should have prevailed among men of education; it seems to have been part of a system, as Mr. Storer, another man of pleasure of the time, specially attended Dr. Dodd's execution, and wrote a lively account of the proceedings, also for the entertainment of his friend Mr. George Selwyn.

Thus ended this tragical history.

IV.

DEATH AT THE FOOTLIGHTS.

As death " visits with equal impartiality the palace of the rich and the hovel of the poor," it is scarcely to be expected that he would stay his hand during the glittering reign of stage delusion. Considering that this covers a period equal to nearly a fifth part of the day, and that in a great city like London so many thousands are concerned in the business,—that the conditions of performing imply labour and much excitement of the nerves and heart, while the heated atmosphere, glaring lights, &c., are scarcely favourable to health, it might be expected that theatrical life would exhibit a more than average death rate. Still, when we think that in spite of the numbers who night after night make up the audiences, how rare is an instance of sudden death, we might be almost tempted to assume that within those charmed portals life was tolerably secure, and that there death was no more a reality than the mimic dissolution witnessed on the stage. It would be scarcely fanciful to ascribe this immunity to a sense of absorbed interest—the grateful occupation of the mind, which suspends, as it were, the advance of decay, or illness; though no doubt many instances could be produced of sudden seizure or death after returning from the theatre. It is certainly pleasant to think that those skilful and hardworking entertainers whose life is devoted to the duty of increasing " the public stock of harmless amusement" should for the most part have found their occupation healthful, and in many instances have reached to an honourable old age. There can be no doubt that " legitimate" histrionic gifts, no matter how laboriously exercised, are favourable to length of life, and that the stage is about as healthful a profession as that of the lawyer.

Many actors have been seized with mortal illness either on the stage or shortly after leaving it, and have survived but a short time. But the instances of death while actually on the stage are very few indeed. The "leading case" is of course that of Palmer,—" Jack Palmer," as he was familiarly styled,—one of the most airy and animated comedians of the English stage—the original Joseph Surface—for whom the part, it is said, was written; and whose naturally insincere character furnished the author with a good many artful touches. His acting too helped Lamb to illustrate his favorite theory, that comedy should be pitched in a key somewhat above the tones of ordinary life—and should not be an accurate reproduction of the manners and the humours of the day. Author and actor, it seemed to him, should pierce to the motives and universal principles of human nature, of which such surface manifestations are merely results—whereas the average realist is no more than a laborious, unintelligent copyist. This passage in the Elia Essays unquestionably contains the true principle of Comedy acting and Comedy writing, and accounts for the failure of so many intelligent writers of our time.

Kotzebue's lugubrious play of 'The Stranger,' after furnishing occasion for another great "creation" to Kemble, had found its way to the provinces, and, in the year 1798, was being acted at Liverpool. Palmer was engaged, and with some inappropriateness had taken the part of the misanthropical hero. Still a comedian of genius might give a very satisfactory interpretation of a tragical character, though an eminent tragedian would scarcely be at home in the comedian's part. In August the theatrical world was shocked with the following account of his sudden death on the stage, which went the round of the papers:—

"DEATH OF JOHN PALMER.

"On the morning of the day on which he was to have performed 'The Stranger,' he received for the first time the distressing intelligence of the death of his second son, a youth in whom his tenderest hopes were centred, and whose amiable manners had brought into action the tenderest affections of a parent. The play, in consequence of this, was deferred; and, during the interval, he had in vain endeavoured to calm the agitation of his mind. The success with which he performed the part called for a second representation, in which he fell a sacrifice to the poignancy of his own feelings, and when the audience were doomed to witness a catastrophe which was truly melancholy.

"In the fourth act, Baron Steinfort obtains an interview with the Stranger, whom he discovers to be his old friend. He prevails on him to relate the cause of his seclusion from the world: in this relation the feelings of Mr. Palmer were visibly much agitated, and at the moment he mentioned his wife and children, having uttered (as in the character), '*there is another and a better world!*' he fell lifeless on the stage. The audience supposed for the moment that his fall was nothing more than a studied addition to the part; but on seeing him carried off in deadly stiffness, the utmost astonishment and terror became depicted in every countenance. Hamerton, Callan, and

Mara were the persons who conveyed the lifeless corpse from the stage into the green-room. Medical assistance was immediately procured; his veins were opened, but they yielded not a single drop of blood, and every other means of resuscitation were had recourse to without effect.

"The gentlemen of the faculty, finding every endeavour ineffectual, formally announced his death; the surgical operations upon the body continued about an hour; after which, all hopes of recovery having vanished, he was carried home to his lodgings on a bier, where a regular inventory was taken of his property. Mr. Aickin, the manager, came on the stage to announce the melancholy event to the audience, but was so completely overcome with grief as to be incapable of uttering a sentence, and was at length forced to retire without being able to make himself understood: he was bathed in tears, and, for the moment, sunk under the generous feelings of his manly nature. Incledon then came forward, and mustered sufficient resolution to communicate the dreadful circumstance. The house was instantly evacuated in mournful silence, and the people, forming themselves into parties, contemplated the fatal occurrence in the open square till a late hour next morning. Doctors Mitchell and Corry gave it as their opinion that he certainly died of a broken heart, in consequence of the family afflictions which he had lately experienced."

This incident was shocking enough, but what peculiarly affected the public mind was the strange coincidence of its occurring after the utterance of the words "there is another and a better world." The party of the community who regarded the stage as a nursery of all that was sinful and demoralising, seized the occasion to point a moral; and were not slow to see in this visitation something of a judgment. It was thought that the actor who would talk with histrionic levity of that "other and better world" to which his profession could not lead him, was appropriately chastised at such a moment,—and that his fate was a warning. This view was urged in pamphlets and from the pulpit; and owing to these exertions the story has become firmly established as a melancholy tradition of the stage.

Much of this dramatic element vanishes when it is ascertained that the event took place at another passage of the piece. The words "another and a better world" occur in the second act; the unfortunate actor had reached the fourth act, and was speaking about the children to Whitfield, who played Baron Steinfort. When he came to the words "I left them at a small town hard by," the memory of his own loss no doubt rushed upon him,—and after some vain attempts to articulate the words, he fell lifeless on the stage. After all, there is something more pathetic in this version.

Mr. Cummins, who, as we have seen, was one of Tate Wilkinson's leading actors, and supposed at York "to read Shakespeare better than any man in England" (and in the provinces performers thus gifted are almost as numerous as that commonly met animal "the best horse in the kingdom"), has been already sketched. Indeed he was considered at York to excel even Barry in sweetness of voice, but, encouraged by the applause of that town, he grew to roar and rant, so that when Kemble came to display his own more regular talents, he was told candidly by the gallery that "he cud na *shoot* oot laik Coomens." In virtue of his popularity he retained all the round of youthful characters, though of good age and great bulk. On the evening of June 20th, 1817, he was playing in 'Jane Shore' at the Leeds Theatre, and in the last scene was uttering the well-known speech—

> "Be witness for me, ye celestial hosts,
> Such mercy, and such pardon, as my soul
> Accords to thee, and begs of Heaven to show thee,
> May such befall me, at my latest hour"—

when he suddenly tottered, sank down and expired. The audience assumed this to be part of the piece, and applauded heartily. Perhaps the poor player's suffering at that moment lent a realism to the performance to which in all his career he had never yet reached. When the news became known the deepest sympathy was felt, and the whole town thrown into commotion. This instance would have been yet more favourable to the theory of "a judgment" put forward by the "saints," and have pointed a moral more effectively than the case of Palmer.

An actor named Bond was, in 1735, playing the old man Lusignan, and while sitting in an arm-chair, had fervently uttered the blessing on his children, set down in his part. When Zara came to reply she found that he had expired in his chair.

Peterson's end had nearly the same appropriateness as Cummins'. In October 1758, when he was playing the Duke in 'Measure for Measure,' with Moody, he came to the words—

> "Reason thus with life:
> If I do lose thee, I do lose a thing
> That none but fools would keep;
> a breath thou art ——"

when he fell into Moody's arms and shortly after expired. He must have been a pleasant creature, to judge by the solitary recorded instance of his humour, which perhaps his sudden end caused to be remembered. He was pressing a brother actor for the repayment of a sum of two shillings, now long due: "Let a fellow alone," was the reply, "I am sure to pay you in some shape or other." Peterson answered good-humouredly, "I shall be obliged to you to let it be as much *like two shillings as you can.*"

His friends placed on his tomb-stone, in St. Edmund's Bury, the last words he uttered.

The latest instance of all is the recent one of Mr. Jordans, a respectable, painstaking actor, who, a few months ago, was struck down when upon the stage.

Seizure by apoplexy or other illness on the stage, shortly followed by death—as in the cases of Peg Woffington, Farren, Harley, Fulham at

Dublin in the year 1826, scarcely fall within this category. The players were advanced in life, and the stage was scarcely connected with the attacks.

"The last night," says the quaint Wilkinson, "Frodsham ever spoke on the stage was in October 1768. After playing Lord Townly, and though in apparent great spirits, he died within three days after :—

"'Ladies and gentlemen, on Monday evening "Coriolanus." To which will be added' (looking seriously, and laying his hand on his heart)

'What we must all come to!'

which expression will serve as a pause to my imperfections and digressions, and afford my reader a leisure for five minutes' reflection."

Several more instances could no doubt be quoted, but these will be found sufficiently typical.*

---

* The reader may be referred, for some curious details of the life behind the curtain, to a series of interesting papers that have lately appeared in 'All the Year Round,' with the following titles :— "Doubles," No. 222 ; "Theatrical Gagging," No. 271 ; "Goose," No. 200 ; "Come the Recorders," No. 146 ; "Stage Whispers," No. 150 ; "In the Pit," No. 154 ; "Bill of the Play," No. 156 ; "Stage Banquets," No. 164 ; "The Super," No. 175 ; "Strolling Players," No. 182 ; and "Stage Wigs," No. 185.

CHAPTER III.

THE IRELAND FORGERIES.*

THE story of the Ireland forgeries is singularly interesting, as exhibiting a *tour de force* second only to the more wonderful attempt of Chatterton. It wants, however, the romantic element, and the piteous issue which almost redeemed the follies of "the marvellous boy,"—beside whose genius and poetical power, the efforts of his imitator sink into a vulgar imposture. The cynic, however, may find a satisfaction in seeing how the Shakespearian critics of the day were duped, such of them, at least, whose pretensions amounted to no more than a vague enthusiasm, and vehement controversial ardour where their notes and commentaries were concerned.

One Samuel Ireland, who had been a Spitalfields silk mercer, had been led to abandon his trade for what was supposed to be antiquarian and literary pursuits, but which was virtually the adoption of a

* Born 1775, died 1835.

new trade. He collected rare old English editions with a view to their resale at large prices, a taste for securing such treasures then becoming fashionable. In these matters he had some knowledge, and a certain enthusiasm, which gave an interest and energy to his pursuit. He also devoted himself to the preparation of pictorial "journeys," illustrated by sepia lithographs, which occasionally turn up on stalls, and which were described at the time as "elegant Tours which may be regarded as works of standard taste." On one of his expeditions to Stratford he brought with him his son William Henry, a lad of sixteen, whom the father's enthusiasm and the sight of the various relics of the place had inspired with quite a Shakespearian glow. By constantly dwelling on the subject, and living in a sort of Shakespearian atmosphere, this feeling soon became a sort of morbid passion or mania—so absorbing as to curiously extinguish all feeling of morality or principle. The young Ireland had heard of Chatterton's story, then recent. The extraordinary interest which had been excited by it had a strange fascination for him. He himself was clever, skilful in shifts and devices of penmanship, and found himself irresistibly drawn to make attempts in the same direction. One trifling success was fatal encouragement. He possessed an old vellum-bound volume, with arms displayed on the covers, and a dedication from the author to Queen Elizabeth. A curious idea occurred to him. He mixed water with his ink to lighten the colour, and on the fly leaf proceeded to compose and write a sort of inscription to the Queen; as though the volume had been a presentation copy. He then brought it to his father, who, he says, was enchanted, and accepted it as genuine. This is his own story, but it will be seen later that it was currently believed that the father was privy to the whole imposture. Greatly encouraged by these praises, he was eager to go on: and the subject of his second attempt shows how reckless and daring he had become even already. He had noticed in a shop window a small terra-cotta bust of Cromwell, which had been rather cleverly executed by some living modeller. He brought it home, pasted a piece of paper on the back with an inscription in sham "old writing" to the effect that it had been "a present to Bradshaw" from the Protector himself. His father again fell into raptures. It was exhibited to the curious. Some of the clever people presently discovered that "it was *in the manner* of Simon," an eminent sculptor of Cromwell's day. But what was regarded as making the authority of the bust certain, was that the handwriting at the back was pronounced to be " wonderfully like Bradshaw's ! "

The young fellow determined to aim at higher game. It was now in the year 1793, and he was just eighteen. He cut off a sheet of parchment from an old deed,—a binder whom he knew had shown him how to mix a more deceptive kind of ink,—and placing some writing of the period before him, he proceeded to prepare a lease between Shakespeare and one Hemminge, duly witnessed and sealed. To insure a difference in the handwriting he wrote the witnesses' name with his left hand. The seal was a more serious difficulty. He tried to melt down some of the seals attached to the old deed, but he found that, instead of softening, when he held them to the fire they were baked away into powder. His ingenuity suggested a better plan. He heated a sharp knife, sliced off the top surface with the impression, and, joining it to a piece of modern wax, inserted the usual piece of ribbon between to attach it to the deed. Having thus completed his task, he walked into his father's room, whom he was always thus surprising, saying, " Sir, I have a great curiosity to show you," then drew it out, and laid it on the table with "There, sir, what do you think of *that!* " The father was astonished and delighted. The curiosity was exhibited to the connoisseurs, and pronounced genuine beyond a doubt. Even the seal (selected at hazard), which bore the impression of a quintain, was found to be a device in some way connected with the Bard, and in a short time it came to be stated with all gravity that this "*was Shakespeare's favourite seal.*" No better satire than this, it may be repeated, could be found on the state of self-delusion to which an immoderate passion may lead the collector. Mr. Pickwick's discovery is even less absurd.

The enthusiasm continued to increase, and numbers arrived every day to inspect the newly discovered treasure. It was tested and criticised in every way, and when there was any difficulty started, it was met by some ready solution. But already his discovery was bringing inconveniences. He was pressed with eager questionings—as to where the treasure had come from : where such a *trouvaille* had been more was certain to be : and forthwith a story had to be cautiously and ingeniously devised. The story was as follows :—It seems there was an old gentleman of antiquarian tastes with whom he had become acquainted at a coffee house, and, who finding out he had an antiquarian taste, mentioned that he had a roomful of old papers, documents, &c., which he was welcome to examine, and also to take away what suited him. The young man had gone, and speedily discovered the precious Shakespearian deed. The old gentleman was a little surprised, but said he would not go back from his word. The young Ireland had also discovered some valuable family papers, and the old gentleman, grateful for the service, was glad to compliment him with a present. This cloudy story was accepted with all faith by the antiquarians, though not without impatience. *What was the name of this wonderful being*, whom they longed to invade? *That*, however, he had been solemnly pledged never to reveal. Presently, no less personages than Dr. Parr and Dr. Warton became interested in the subject, and curious to see the relics. There was not much, after all, to show such important people: but his father was pressing him to make fresh inquiries and searches; such remissness was culpable. So within a short time a "Profession of Faith" of a Protestant character was discovered in Shakespeare's own handwriting. This treasure, it was announced,

Doctors Parr and Warton were coming to see. He began to feel nervous, and would have given, he owns, anything to avoid the meeting. The document was inspected and read out, and to his amazement the great Dr. Parr said gravely, "Sir, we have very fine passages in our Services, *but here is one who has distanced us all!*" No wonder that his vanity was inflamed by so genuine a compliment. *His* work taken for Shakespere's and by such judges! After this it is to be feared that not many antiquaries are able to withstand the seduction of an antique diction, or of antique writing, material, and other delusive elements.

Again the amateurs were pressing him to make fresh searches. His indifference was impatiently tolerated, and he was almost forced to manufacture a few trifles to stay their appetites. He discovered "the witty conundrum of Shakespere to Maister Cowley," a bit of nonsensical doggerel in which, to his surprise, the admiring commentators discovered much point and significance, though, as he confesses, he had no distinct idea in his head. Growing bolder, he next discovered "a letter to Anne Hathaway,"—and as he was completing it, it occurred to him that a lock of hair would be a dramatic inclosure. He bethought him of such a souvenir given him by an old flame. The modern thread with which it was tied up was a difficulty; but his artful enthusiasm was prepared, and he drew a thread out of the tapestry in the House of Lords, which was ancient enough. The hair was unanimously pronounced to answer to the traditions of the Shakespearian hair, was reverentially kissed, and portions of it set in rings.

All this time, however, he had a presentiment of danger. Mr. Albany Wallis—who was Garrick's solicitor, and a shrewd intelligent man—discovered among some old deeds, a signature of John Hemminge's, Shakespeare's lessee. He sent for Ireland and showed him that the signature did not in the least resemble the fictitious one. Here was an awkward discovery. The young man felt his heart sink, but had composure enough to say that it was very strange, but he thought that he could clear the matter up. As he was walking home he devised a scheme: then sat down, and from memory imitated the signature that had just been shown to him and attached it to a receipt. He then repaired to Mr. Wallis and told this story: He had been to the old gentleman, and related the curious discovery that had been made, when the latter "shook his head with meaning, and smilingly said, 'Take *that* to Mr. Wallis.'" How could Mr. Wallis know that there were *two* Hemminges, "one of the Globe, the other of the Curtain Theatre"? The Globe actor was distinguished as "tall John Hemminge," the Curtain actor as "short John." This elaborate falsehood was hurriedly fabricated during the few minutes that he was walking home; and it shows that his mind had a natural bent in the direction of deceit. The explanation was accepted and the danger, for the present, escaped.

Some of these freaks were no doubt prompted by a desire to victimise the antiquarian gulls, whose ignorance was really inviting deception. Thus he chanced to see an old Dutch portrait in a curiosity shop. He put a pair of scales into the hand and added W. S. in the corner. He had only to announce that it came from the old gentleman's magazine, and the antiquarians recognised it as the immortal Bard himself "in the character of Shylock!" "It had probably been hung up in the green-room," in compliment to "Maister Shakespere!" Other "relics" were produced from time to time, and the "curious" came in such crowds, that particular days in the week were announced by advertisement when they would be exhibited in Norfolk Street. A declaration of belief in the authenticity of the papers was drawn up by the crafty father, which visitors supposed to be judges were invited to sign: and later, to such a declaration were found attached the names of Dr. Parr, Herbert Croft, Duke of Somerset, Garter King at Arms, Boswell, and others. Mr. Boswell took the matter up with his usual enthusiasm, and, kneeling down, thanked God that he had lived to see that day. Porson, however, excused himself with the pleasant remark that he detested signing *articles* of any description, especially *articles of faith*.

It was scarcely wonderful that, with such encouragement, a still bolder step should have been taken. Hitherto there had been much credit, a good deal of reputation, but no profit. The Irelands were little more than dealers in literary curiosities, and there was no reason why the Bard should not be made to bring pecuniary advantages. Surprise had often been expressed that in such a treasury of old papers no PLAY had been discovered. The poet must surely have left behind him, in company with the other scraps, some rude sketches of scenes, acts—or possibly an entire drama, which had been rejected as not quite up to his standard.

This was like an invitation, and soon hints were thrown out that the investigator was on the track. Presently the antiquarians were thrown into a delirium of joy by learning that a tragedy entitled VORTIGERN and ROWENA, by W. Shakespere, had been recovered.

No time was lost. Offers were received from the managers. One from Harris of Covent Garden was declined, one from Sheridan of Drury Lane was accepted. That versatile genius had his suspicions, and was staggered by the prosy and un-Shakespearian character of many of the lines. Indeed he was said to have declared to some friends that the piece might no doubt have been Shakespeare's work, but that he must have been *drunk* when he wrote it. Three hundred pounds was to be paid for the treasure, and the profits of the first sixty nights of performance divided between the sponsors and the manager. Great expense was gone to for scenery, and the parts allotted to Kemble and other important performers.

But it was felt that this was going too far. A few men of real critical sagacity, such as Malone and Steevens, were persuaded by a sort of instinct that such "discoveries" were *à priori* impossible, or inconsistent with what their own labours had taught them. Reed, Farmer, Ritson, Percy, and Douglas, the Bishop of Salisbury (who had already exposed another imposture, Lauder's) denounced the whole as a monstrous forgery. These names carried more weight than those of amateurs like Garter King at Arms, the impulsive Boswell, or even the eccentric Parr. The specimens furnished, to be followed by others, placed the discoveries in fatally convenient shape for sober investigation and critical testing; and Malone flung himself on these with professional ardour and merciless severity.*

An ordinary reader would see that this was but a *réchauffé* of Portia's speech. And indeed it was upon this principle that the fabrication had proceeded, working in Shakespearian phrases and allusions, in absolute dearth of inspiration. But Malone showed with overwhelming force the blunders into which the writer had fallen. The letter was addressed to "Anne Hathirrewaye," whereas the old spelling is invariably Hathaway. There was no "For" or "To" preceding the name,

---

* He took, for instance, the letter to Anne Hathaway, which ran:— "No rude hande hath knotteddc itte. Thye Willys alone hathe done the worke. Neytherre the gyldedde bawble thatto envyronnes the heade of majestye, noe norre honoures most weyghtye wulde give me halfe the joye as didde thysso myo lyttle worke forre thee."

the usual form of superscription; the "gyldedde Bawble," he showed could not have been Shakespeare's phrase—who always spoke of the "Crown," simply—while his loyalty would have forbidden him such a phrase. These objections, and many more, he embodied in a masterly exposure.*

His labours took the shape of a "letter to the Lord Charlemont, in which it is proved from orthography, phraseology, dates given, or deducible by inference, and dissimilitude of handwriting, that not a single paper or deed in this extraordinary volume was written or executed by the person to whom it was ascribed." Edmund Burke paid the work the odd compliment "that he had got to the seventy-third page before he went to sleep,"—but justly declared that in it "was revived the spirit of that sort of criticism by which false pretence and imposture are detected," and which had grown so rare in England.

This "enquiry" appeared at an awkward moment for the fabricators—on the very eve of the per-

* Indeed, it is hard to resist a smile on looking at these attempts, which suggest the conventional old English with which historical novelists attempt to reproduce the times of King Hal and Queen Bess. An inscription said to have been found at the beginning of a copy of 'King Lear' ran thus:—"The Tragedy of Kynge Lear isse fromme Masterre Hollineshedde. I have inne somme lyttle departedde fromme hymme, butte thatte libbertye wille notte I truste be blammedde by myc gentle readerres."

formance. It was found necessary to distribute a handbill at the doors, which ran :—

" VORTIGERN.

"A malevolent and impudent attack on the Shakespeare MSS. having appeared on the eve of representation of the play of ' Vortigern,' evidently intended to injure the interest of the proprietor of the MSS., Mr. Ireland feels it impossible, within the short space of time that intervenes between the publishing and the representation, to produce an answer to the most illiberal and unfounded assertions in Mr. Malone's enquiry. He is therefore induced to request that the play of ' Vortigern ' may be heard with that candour which has ever distinguished a British audience."

This of course tended to increase the excitement, which about the doors of the theatre was enormous: opposition handbills being distributed, describing the piece as "a rank forgery." It was evident, however, that serious perils were in store for it, both before and behind the scenes. Kemble was in one of those grim humours which are favourite weaknesses of great tragedians, and had shown a marked hostility from the beginning. He had, as it were, washed his hands of the business: and when the sponsor (or author) begged that he would use his judgment in preparing the piece for the stage, the reply he received was that " it should be acted faithfully from the copy sent to the theatre." He was no doubt encouraged by the success of a similar fit of ill-humour only a few nights before. The parts, it was said, had been distributed with studious effort to make the piece as ineffective as possible. Mrs. Siddons had finally declined the heroine, believing the whole to be "an audacious imposture."

Inside, the house presented an extraordinary scene. It was crammed to the roof, while conspicuous in a centre box was the Ireland party. Many had paid box prices, when no seats were to be obtained, for the purpose of getting down into the pit. The air was charged with the murmurs of contending factions, and the partisans and concoctors of the fraud felt uneasy presentiments. The performance began. The young fabricator was behind the scenes, nervous, agitated, but received kindly encouragement from the good-natured Jordan, who performed in the piece.

With occasional signs of disapprobation, all went fairly for a couple of acts. But the opponents were only reserving their powers. The absurdities of some of the actors then came in aid, and were greeted with derision: as when Dignum, a pleasing singer, but no actor, gave out in a guttural croak an invitation to the trumpets, "Let them *bellow* on!" it was not unnaturally greeted with a shout of laughter; or when Mr. Philimore, a comic performer with a large nose, who had been fitted with the part of "the Saxon general, Horsus," was killed in due course, fresh amusement was produced by his dying agonies. As the drop-scene descended, the heavy roller rested on his chest, and it was some time before he could be extricated, his groans reaching the audience, and convulsing the house with merriment. But Kemble contributed most to the general "damnation": all through he had preserved a stolid and conscientious bearing, not making the least exertion, but delivering the lines in a funereal fashion. As he spoke various Shakespearian passages, the audience, with unusual intelligence, would call out, "Henry IV.," "Othello," or whatever play the line was stolen from.* But at last it went beyond endurance, and Kemble gave the

---

* The mock stuff was, however, ingeniously put together, as in the passages :—

"Give me a sword!
I have so clogg'd and badged this with blood
And slippery gore, that it doth mock my grasp."

signal for the *coup de grâce* by his delivering of some lines on death:—

> "O thou that dost ope wide thy hideous jaws,
> And with rude laughter and fantastic tricks
> Thou clappest thy rattling fingers to thy side—
> *And when this solemn mockery is o'er—*"

Here one universal shout pointed the application of the speech, and a chorus of groans, catcalls, and the usual hurricane of theatrical disapprobation sealed the fate of the play. As soon as there was a lull, Kemble, with a cruel iteration, slowly and lugubriously repeated the line—

> "And when this solemn mockery is o'er,"

which provoked a fresh howl, and the whole closed in confusion.

The play was of course never acted again, though the fabricator was paid on the following morning. Notwithstanding this rude shock, the impostors proceeded in their task with even more confidence. The book had appeared, a magnificent volume, full of illustrations and facsimiles, and sold at an enormous price. Even now it excites wonder, from the ingenuity and elaborateness with which the deception is carried out. Had it appeared before the play, it would have brought in a splendid sum to the concocters. But more than suspicion had been aroused. A loud clamour arose that the name of the mysterious old gentleman, the owner of the treasures, should be given up. A committee was appointed to examine the question, which suggested that two of their number should be selected who were to be informed of the gentleman's name, and sworn to secrecy. In an agony of doubt, the wretched young fellow knew not what course to take, and at last bethought him of throwing himself on the generosity of Mr. Albany Wallis, the solicitor, and confessing the whole story to him. He was naturally amazed at the revelation. Ireland asked him what was to be done. He good-naturedly promised to keep silence, and would give out that the gentleman did not consider it safe to trust his secret to the public. Still this was only staving the matter off. At last, pressed and harassed on all sides, the youth fled from home, and swore an affidavit before a magistrate, clearing his father, who had been attacked by Malone; then, after an absence returned to his father to confess the whole. The father, he says, was inexpressibly astonished, and could not believe the story; then, affected to cast him off altogether as an impostor.

Such is the story told by the young man himself in his curious "confessions." It will be seen that the object was to enlist sympathy, as in the case of Chatterton, for a youth lamentably led astray, but with a genius and cleverness that deserved indulgence.

But Steevens and others were not to be thus imposed upon. It was believed that the father, an old hand at such fabrications, had been the chief contriver, and that the house in Northumberland Street was no more than an elaborate workshop, in which the whole family laboured. The quarrel between the father and son, was supposed to have been got up with a view "of whitewashing the father," whose business it would have fatally destroyed.*

A volume which he had issued, containing designs by Hogarth, long considered to be spurious, was recollected. He was also a collector of books belonging to the Shakespearian era, which he decorated with fabricated inscriptions on the

* Steevens to Bishop Percy. See also note in 'Willis' Current Notes,' from a gentleman well acquainted with the family.

fly-leaves and margins, and sold as rarities. This seemed almost conclusive, or at least more probable than that a lad of sixteen should have shown such precocious ability. A daughter was said to have laboured at the forged autographs. Finally, as Ireland had showed deceit in the imposition, his elaborate " confessions" might be equally open to the charge of being untruthful.

The rest of the story is uninteresting. He is said to have become a sort of hack writer, and died, in the year 1835, in miserable circumstances.

CHAPTER IV.

MRS. ROBINSON.

CLOSE to the Bristol cathedral used to stand a mansion, half a ruin, half a modern restoration, in which the well-known heroine Mary Darby, or Robinson, or "Perdita," was born. "In this awe-inspiring habitation," she says in her high-flown memoirs, "which I shall henceforth denominate the Minster-house, during a tempestuous night, on the twenty-seventh of November, 1758, I first opened my eyes to this world of duplicity and sorrow. I have often heard my mother say that a more stormy hour she never remembered. The wind whistled round the dark pinnacles of the minster tower, and the rain beat in torrents against the casements of her chamber. Through life the tempest has followed my footsteps, and I have in vain looked for a short interval of repose from the perseverance of sorrow."

From this introduction, a fair idea may be

* Born 1758, died 1800.

gathered of the melodramatic nature of the fair creature who is about to relate her adventures. Beautiful, interesting, romantic, persecuted by those who should have protected her, pursued by wicked men, and further, abandoned by the faithless lover who had led her astray, her story reads like some agonizing heroine's in the old romances. And though the life of one so frail as well as so fair, is to be sternly judged according to the conventional law of society, it will be seen that some allowance must be made for her position. Her family was of Irish origin, and formerly bore the name of Macdermott, which was changed to that of Darby; her father, "a man of strong mind, high spirit, and great personal intrepidity," was half an American, and all his life addicted to speculations and pleasure. When his little girl Mary was at a school kept by the Misses More, sisters of the famous Hannah, he conceived a vast Quixotic scheme of founding a great fishing settlement on the Labrador, and set off for America to arrange for carrying it out. His wife and family were left behind in England. After three years' absence he returned, nearly all his fortune having been swallowed up through the Indians having destroyed the settlement. He then deserted his family, his wife having been compelled to open a small school, so as to earn means for the support of herself and her children. On this intelligence reaching him, he characteristically became angry at what he considered was a degradation to his name, and insisted on the school being broken up.

His daughter Mary, then about fourteen or fifteen years old, and showing great signs of beauty and intelligence, had been taking some lessons in dancing from a master who was connected with Covent Garden Theatre. This Professor was so struck with her intelligence that he spoke of her to one of the actors. Mr. Garrick, who was then retiring from the stage, was later induced to allow her to exhibit before him, and was so delighted that he proposed that she should appear with him. But these dazzling plans were interrupted by a more important matter.

A gentleman who constantly appeared at the opposite window, and showed signs of his admiration, attracted her. " One evening, a party of six was proposed for the following Sunday; with much persuasion my mother consented to go, and to allow that I should also attend her. Greenwich was the place fixed on for the dinner; and we prepared for the day of recreation. It was then the fashion to wear silks. I remember that I wore a nightgown of pale blue lustring, with a chip hat, trimmed with ribbands of the same colour. Never was I dressed so perfectly to my own satisfaction: I anticipated a day of admiration; Heaven can bear witness that, to me, it was a day of fatal victory!

"On our stopping at the Star and Garter, at Greenwich, the person who came to hand me from the carriage was our opposite neighbour in Southampton Buildings. I was confused; but my mother was indignant! Mr. Wayman presented his young friend—that friend who was ordained to be MY HUSBAND.

"Our party dined; and early in the evening we returned to London. Mr. Robinson remained at Greenwich for the benefit of the air, being recently recovered from a fit of sickness. During the remainder of the evening, Mr. Wayman expatiated on the many good qualities of his friend Mr. Robinson, spoke of his future expectations from a rich old uncle, of his probable advancement in his profession, and, more than all, of his enthusiastic admiration of me.

"A few days after, Mr. Robinson paid my mother a visit. We had now removed to Villiers Street,

York Buildings. My mother's fondness for books of a moral and religious character was not lost upon my new lover; and elegantly bound editions of Hervey's Meditations, with some others of a similar description, were presented, as small tokens of admiration and respect. My mother was beguiled by these little interesting attentions, and soon began to feel a strong predilection in favour of Mr. Robinson."

During the illness that followed, Mr. Robinson was so devoted that a consent was at last extorted and the marriage took place :—the bride being so youthful that only three months before she had given up dressing her dolls. To her great surprise Mr. Robinson insisted that the matter should be kept secret, owing to family reasons, and to a fear of displeasing a firm of attorneys to whom he was articled. After a short time she began to have suspicions, and it was insisted that the bride should be taken to see the important uncle in Wales, to whom her husband gave out that he was heir—but whose illegitimate son he in reality was; unable to make further excuses, he consented, and both set off for Wales, and arrived at Mr. Harris' house.

"Mr. Harris came out to receive me. I wore a

dark claret-coloured riding-habit, with a white beaver hat and feathers. He embraced me with excessive cordiality, while Miss Robinson, my husband's sister, with cold formality led me into the house. I never shall forget her looks or her manner. Had her brother presented the most abject being to her, she could not have taken my hand with a more frigid demeanour. Miss Robinson, though not more than twenty years of age, was Gothic in her appearance, and stiff in her deportment; she was of low stature, and clumsy, with a countenance peculiarly formed for the expression of sarcastic vulgarity—a short snub nose, turned up at the point, a head thrown back with an air of *hauteur*, a gaudy-coloured chintz gown, a thrice-bordered cap, with a profusion of ribbands, and a countenance somewhat more ruddy than was consistent with even pure health, presented the personage whom I was to know as my future companion and kinswoman!

" Mr. Harris looked like a venerable Hawthorn; a brown fustian coat, a scarlet waistcoat edged with narrow gold, a pair of woollen spatter-dashes, and a gold-laced hat, formed the dress he generally wore. He always rode a small Welsh pony; and was seldom in the house, excepting at meal-time, from sunrise to the close of evening.

"There was yet another personage in the domestic establishment, who was by Mr. Harris regarded as of no small importance: this was a venerable housekeeper, of the name of Mary Edwards. Mrs. Molly was the female Mentor of the family; she dined at the table with Mr. Harris; she was the governess of the domestic department: and a more overbearing, vindictive spirit never inhabited the heart of mortal, than that which pervaded the soul of the ill-natured Mrs. Molly.

"It may easily be conjectured that my time passed heavily in this uninteresting circle. I was condemned either to drink ale with 'the Squire,' for Mr. Harris was only spoken of by that title, or to visit the Methodistical seminary which Lady Huntingdon had established at Trevecca, another mansion-house on the estate of Mr. Harris. Miss Robinson was of this sect; and though Mr. Harris was not a disciple of the Huntingdonian School, he was a constant church visitor on every Sunday. His zeal was indefatigable; and he would frequently fine the rustics (for he was a justice of the peace, and had been sheriff of the county) when he heard them swear, though every third sentence he uttered was attended by an oath that made his hearers shudder.

"I soon became a considerable favourite with the *Squire;* but I did not find any yielding qualities about the hearts of Miss Betsy or Mrs. Molly. They observed me with jealous eyes; they considered me as an interloper, whose manner attracted Mr. Harris's esteem, and who was likely to diminish their divided influence in the family. I found them daily growing weary of my society; I perceived their sidelong glances when I was complimented by the visiting neighbours on my good looks, or taste in the choice of my dresses. Miss Robinson rode on horseback in a camlet safe-guard, with a high-crowned bonnet. I wore a fashionable habit, and looked like something human. Envy at length assumed the form of insolence, and I was taunted perpetually on the folly of appearing like a woman of fortune; that a lawyer's wife had no right to dress like a duchess; and that, though I might be very accomplished, a good housewife had no occasion for harpsichords and books; they belonged to women who brought wherewithal to support them. Such was the language of vulgar illiberal natures! yet for three weeks I endured it patiently.

"Knowing that Mr. Harris was disposed to think favourably of me—that he even declared he should 'have liked me for his wife, had I not *married Tom*,' though he was then between sixty and seventy years of age, I thought it most prudent to depart, lest through the machinations of Miss Betsy and Mrs. Molly I should lose the share I had gained in his affections. My mother was still at Bristol; and the morning of our departure being arrived, to my infinite astonishment, Mr. Harris proposed accompanying us thither. It was in vain that Molly and Miss interfered to prevent him; he swore that he would see me safe across the Channel, whatever might be the consequence of his journey. We set out together.

"After passing many days at Bristol, Mr. Harris returned to Wales, and our party set out for London. Mr. Robinson's mind was easy, and his hopes were confirmed by the kindness of his uncle: he now considered himself as the most happy of mortals. We removed from Great Queen Street, to a house, No. 13, in Hatton Garden, which had been recently built. Mr. Robinson hired it, and furnished it with peculiar elegance. I frequently inquired into the extent of his finances, and he as often assured me that they were in every respect competent to his expenses. In addition to our domestic establishment, Mr. Robinson purchased a handsome phaeton, with saddle horses for his own use: and I now made my *début*, though scarcely emerged beyond the boundaries of childhood, in the broad hemisphere of fashionable folly.

"A new face, a young person dressed with peculiar but simple elegance, was sure to attract attention at places of public entertainment. The first time I went to Ranelagh my habit was so singularly plain and quaker-like, that all eyes were fixed upon me. I wore a gown of light brown lustring with close round cuffs (it was then the fashion to wear long ruffles); my hair was without powder, and my head adorned with a plain round cap and a white chip hat, without any ornaments whatever.

"The second place of polite entertainment, to which Mr. Robinson accompanied me, was the Pantheon Concert, then the most fashionable assemblage of the gay and the distinguished. At this place it was customary to appear much dressed; large hoops and high feathers were universally worn.

"As soon as I entered the Pantheon Rotunda, I never shall forget the impression which my mind received: the splendour of the scene, the dome illuminated with variegated lamps, the music, and the beauty of the women, seemed to present a circle of enchantment. I recollect that the most lovely of fair forms met my eyes in that of Lady Almeria Carpenter. The countenance which most pleased me was that of the late Mrs. Baddeley. The first Countess of Tyrconnel also appeared with considerable *éclat*. But the buzz of the room, the unceasing murmur of admiration, attended the Marchioness of Townshend. I took my seat on a sofa nearly opposite to that on which she was sitting, and I observed two persons, evidently men of fashion, speaking to her; till one of them, looking towards me, with an audible voice inquired of the other 'Who is she?'

"Their fixed stare disconcerted me. I rose, and leaning on my husband's arm, again mingled in the brilliant circle. The inquirers followed us, stopping several friends, as we walked round the circle, and repeatedly demanding of them, 'Who is that young lady in the pink dress trimmed with sable?' My manner and confusion plainly evinced that I was not accustomed to the gaze of impertinent high breeding. I felt uneasy, and proposed returning home, when I perceived that our two followers were joined by a third, who, on looking at me, said, 'I think I know her.' It was the late Earl of Northington.

"We had now to pass the group in order to quit the rotunda. Lord Northington, leaving his companions, approached me. 'Miss Darby, or I am mistaken,' said he, with a bow of marked civility. I replied that my name was now changed to that of Robinson: and, to prevent any awkward embarrassment, presented my husband, on whose arm I was still leaning. Lord Northington continued to walk round the Pantheon with us, made many inquiries after my father, complimented me on the improvement of my person, and hoped that he should be permitted to pay his respects to Mr. and Mrs. Robinson.

"We now entered the tea-room: there was not a seat vacant: I was considerably fatigued, and somewhat faint with the heat of the rotunda. I quitted the tea-room, and seated myself on a sofa near the door. In a few minutes Lord Northington brought me a cup of tea, for Mr. Robinson did not like to leave me alone; and at the same time presented his two inquisitive friends, Lord Lyttelton and Captain Ayscough.

"I now proposed departing. Mr. Robinson accompanied me to the vestibule; and while he was seeking the carriage Lord Lyttelton offered his services. I had never till that evening heard his name; but there was an easy effrontery in his address that completely disgusted me, while his determined gaze distressed and embarrassed me; and I felt inexpressible satisfaction when Mr. Robinson returned to tell me that the carriage was ready. On the following morning Lords Northington, Lyttelton, and Colonel Ayscough made their visits of ceremony. Mr. Robinson was not at home, but I received them, though not without some embarrassment. I was yet a child, and wholly unacquainted with the manners of the world. Yet, young as I was, I became the traveller of its mazy and perilous paths; at an age when girls are generally at school, or indeed scarcely emancipated from the nursery, I was presented in society as a wife—and very nearly as a mother. Lord Lyttelton who was perhaps the most accomplished libertine that any age or country has produced, with considerable artifice inquired after

Mr. Robinson, professed his earnest desire to cultivate his acquaintance, and on the following day sent him a card of invitation. Fortunately for me, Lord Lyttelton was uniformly my aversion. His manners were overbearingly insolent, his language licentious, and his person slovenly even to a degree that was disgusting. Mr. Robinson was in every respect the very reverse of his companion: he was unassuming, neat and delicate in his conversation. I had not a wish to descend from the propriety of wedded life ; and I abhorred, decidedly abhorred, the acquaintance with Lord Lyttelton.

"In the course of a few days his Lordship presented me the works of Miss Aikin, now Mrs. Barbauld: I read them with rapture: I thought them the most beautiful poems I had ever seen ; and considered the woman who could invent such poetry, as the most to be envied of human creatures. Lord Lyttelton had some taste for poetical compositions, and wrote verses with considerable facility.

"On the following Monday, I again visited the Pantheon. My dress was then white and silver. Again I was followed with attention. Lord Lyttelton was my *cavaliere servente* that evening ;

though, as usual, his chief attention was paid to Mr. Robinson. During the concert, he presented the Count de Belgioso, the Imperial Ambassador, one of the most accomplished foreigners I ever remember to have met. Lord Valentia was also introduced; but, as his Lordship had recently made some *éclat* by his attentions to the celebrated Mrs. Elliot, I rather avoided than wished to cultivate his acquaintance.

"Mr. Robinson's intercourse with the world was now rapidly augmenting. Every day was productive of some new association. Lord Lyttelton presented many of his friends: among others Captain O'Byrne, and Mr. William Brereton of Drury Lane Theatre. In the course of a short time we also became acquainted with Sir Francis Molyneux, Mr. Alderman Sayer, and the late unfortunate George Robert Fitzgerald. Lord Northington was also a constant visitor, and frequently rallied me on what he thought my striking likeness to his family.

"I soon discovered that his intercourse with Lord Lyttelton produced a very considerable change in Mr. Robinson's domestic deportment. They were constantly together, and the neglect which I experienced began to alarm me. I dedicated all my leisure hours to poetry: I wrote verses of all sorts; and Mr. Robinson having mentioned that I had purposed appearing on the stage previous to my marriage, in the character of Cordelia, Lord Lyttelton facetiously christened me the Poetess Corry.

"It was with extreme regret, and frequently with uncontrollable indignation, that I endured the neglect of my husband and the tauntings of the profligate Lyttelton—'The child,' for so he generally called me, was deserted for the society of the most libertine men and the most abandoned women. Mr. Robinson became not only careless of his wife, but of his pecuniary concerns; while I was kept in total ignorance as to the resources which supplied his increasing expenses.

"Among the most dangerous of my husband's associates was George Robert Fitzgerald. His manners towards women were interesting and attentive: he perceived the neglect with which I was treated by Mr. Robinson, and the pernicious influence which Lord Lyttelton had acquired over his mind: he professed to feel the warmest interest in my welfare, lamented the destiny which had befallen me, in being wedded to a man incapable of estimating my value, and at last confessed *himself* my most ardent and devoted admirer. I shuddered at the declaration, for amidst all the allurements of splendid folly, my mind, the purity of my virtue, was still uncontaminated.

"I repulsed the dangerous advances of this accomplished person; but I did not the less feel the humiliation to which a husband's indifference had exposed me. God can bear witness to the purity of my soul; even surrounded by temptations, and mortified by neglect. Whenever I ventured to inquire into pecuniary resources, Mr. Robinson silenced me by saying he was independent: added to this assurance, Lord Lyttelton repeatedly promised that, through his courtly interest, he would very shortly obtain for my husband some honourable and lucrative situation.

"I confess that I reposed but little confidence in the promises of such a man, though my husband believed them inviolable. Frequent parties were made at his Lordship's house in Hill Street, and many invitations pressed for a visit to his seat at Hagley. These I peremptorily refused; till the noble hypocrite became convinced of my aversion, and adopted a new mode of pursuing his machinations.

"One forenoon Lord Lyttelton called in Hatton

Garden, as was almost his daily custom; and, on finding that Mr. Robinson was not at home, requested to speak with me on business of importance. I found him seemingly much distressed. He informed me that he had a secret to communicate of considerable moment both to my interest and happiness. I started: 'Nothing, I trust in heaven, has befallen my husband!' said I, with a voice scarcely articulate. Lord Lyttelton hesitated. 'How little does that husband deserve the solicitude of such a wife!' said he; 'but,' continued his Lordship, 'I fear that I have in some degree aided in alienating his conjugal affections. I could not bear to see such youth, such merit, so sacrificed.' 'Speak briefly, my Lord,' said I. 'Then,' replied Lord Lyttelton, 'I must inform you that your husband is the most false and undeserving of that name!' . . .

"'I do not believe it,' said I, indignantly. 'Then you shall be convinced,' answered his Lordship—'but remember, if you betray your true and zealous friend, I must fight your husband; for he never will forgive my having discovered his infidelity.'

"'It cannot be true,' said I. 'You have been misinformed.'

"'Hear me,' said he. 'You cannot be a stranger to my motives for thus cultivating the friendship of your husband: my fortune is at your disposal. Robinson is a ruined man; his debts are considerable, and nothing but destruction can await you. Leave him! Command my powers to serve you.'

"I would hear no more—my hours were all dedicated to sorrow; for I now heard that my husband even at the period of his marriage, had an attachment which he had not broken; and that his infidelities were as public as the ruin of his finances was inevitable. I remonstrated—I was almost frantic. My distress was useless; my wishes to retrench our expenses were ineffectual. Lord Lyttelton now rested his only hope in the certainty of my husband's ruin. He therefore took every step and embraced every opportunity to involve him more deeply in calamity. Parties were made to Richmond and Salthill, to Ascot Heath and Epsom races; in all of which Mr. Robinson bore his share of expense, with the addition of post-horses. Whenever he seemed to shrink from his augmenting indiscretion, Lord Lyttelton assured him that, through his interest, an appointment of honourable and pecuniary importance should be obtained: though I embraced every opportunity to assure his Lordship that no consideration upon earth should ever make me the victim of his artifice.

"Mr. Fitzgerald still paid me unremitting attention His manners *towards women* were beautifully interesting. He frequently cautioned me against the libertine Lyttelton, and as frequently lamented the misguided confidence which Mr. Robinson reposed in him.

" About this time a party was one evening made to Vauxhall. Mr. Fitzgerald was the person who proposed it, and it consisted of six or eight persons. The night was warm, and the gardens crowded; we supped in the circle which has the statue of Handel in its centre. The hour growing late, or rather early in the morning, our company dispersed, and no one remained excepting Mr. Robinson, Mr. Fitzgerald, and myself. Suddenly a noise was heard near the orchestra; a crowd had assembled, and two gentlemen were quarrelling furiously. Mr. R. and Fitzgerald ran out of the box. I rose to follow them, but they were lost in the throng, and I thought it most prudent to resume my place, which I had just quitted, as the only certain way of their finding me in safety. In a moment Fitzgerald returned: 'Robinson,' said he, 'is gone to seek you at the entrance-door; he thought you had quitted the box.' 'I did for a moment,' said I, 'but I was fearful of losing him in the crowd, and therefore returned.'

"'Let me conduct you to the door; we shall certainly find him there,' replied Mr. Fitzgerald: 'I know that he will be uneasy.' I took his arm, and we ran hastily towards the entrance-door on the Vauxhall Road.

"Mr. Robinson was not there: we proceeded to look for our carriage, it stood at some distance. I was alarmed and bewildered. Mr. Fitzgerald hurried me along. 'Don't be uneasy, we shall certainly find him,' said he, 'for I left him here not five minutes ago.' As he spoke he stopped abruptly: a servant opened a chaise door; there were four horses harnessed to it: and, by the light of the lamps on the side of the foot-path, I plainly perceived a pistol in the pocket of the door, which was open. I drew back. Mr. Fitzgerald placed his arm round my waist, and endeavoured to lift me up the step of the chaise; the servant watching at a little distance. I resisted, and inquired what he meant by such conduct; his hand trembled excessively, while he said in a low voice: 'Robinson can but fight me.' I was terrified beyond all description :—I made him loose his hold—and ran towards the entrance door. Mr. Fitzgerald now perceived Mr. Robinson. 'Here he comes!' exclaimed he with an easy *nonchalance.* 'We had found the wrong carriage, Mr. Robinson: we have been looking after you, and Mrs. Robinson is alarmed beyond expression.'

'I am indeed!' said I. Mr. Robinson now took my hand. We stepped into the coach, and Mr. Fitzgerald followed. As we proceeded towards Hatton Garden, the sky incessantly flashed lightning. I was terrified by the combination of events; and I was in a situation which rendered any alarm peculiarly dangerous, for I was several months advanced in that state which afterwards terminated by presenting to me my only child— my *darling* MARIA.

" I had often heard of Mr. Fitzgerald's propensity to duelling—I recollected my own delicate situation—I valued my husband's safety, I therefore did not mention the adventure of the evening: particularly as Mr. Fitzgerald observed, in our way to Hatton Garden, that he had 'nearly made a strange mistake, and taken possession of another person's carriage.' This remark appeared so plausible that nothing further was said upon the subject.

"From that evening I was particularly cautious in avoiding Fitzgerald. He was too daring, and too fascinating a being, to be allowed the smallest marks of confidence. Whenever he called, I was denied to him: and at length, perceiving the impracticability of his plan, he desisted, and seldom called excepting to leave his name, as a visitor of ceremony.

"I do not recount these events, these plans for my enthralment, with a view to convey anything like personal vanity; for I can with truth affirm that I never thought myself entitled to admiration that could endanger my security.

"I was now known, by name, at every public place in and near the metropolis: our circle of acquaintances enlarged daily; my friend Lady Yea was my constant companion. Mr. Robinson became desperate, from a thorough conviction that no effort of economy or professional labour could arrange his shattered finances: the large debt which he owed *previous to his marriage with me*, having laid the foundation for every succeeding embarrassment.

"The moment now approached when the arcanum

was to be developed; and an execution on Mr. Robinson's effects, at the suit of an annuitant, decided the doubts and fears which had long afflicted me. I was in a great degree prepared for this event, by the evident inquietude of my husband's mind, and his frequent interviews with persons of a mysterious description. Indeed this crisis seemed rather consolatory than appalling."

After many trials and humiliations she went to the country, but soon came back to London. She brought a small collection of poems with her, which she intended publishing, and her "sweet Maria." A few days after her arrival she was induced again to visit Ranalagh, when the persevering Mr. Fitzgerald and odious Lyttelton again pursued her with their attentions. Her husband was almost at once arrested, and his beautiful wife took up her abode with him in the prison. There seemed to be no prospect of extrication, when the idea of the stage again recurred. Friends assisted; she was introduced to Sheridan, who affected to be astonished by her powers, though he was more probably calculating what an addition such a fascinating creature would be to the ranks of his actresses. Mr. Robinson, who possessed more than the average ingenuity and shifts of needy men, soon obtained his release, and the matter was now pushed forward with great zeal and earnestness.

"The only objection which I felt to the idea of appearing on the stage was my then increasing state of domestic solicitude. I was, at the period when Mr. Sheridan was first presented to me, some months advanced in that situation which afterwards, by the birth of Sophia, made me a second time a mother. Yet such was my imprudent fondness for Maria that I was still a nurse; and my constitution was very considerably impaired by the effects of these combining circumstances.

"An appointment was made in the green-room of Drury-Lane Theatre. Mr. Garrick, Mr. Sheridan, Mr. Brereton, and my husband were present; I there recited the principal scenes of Juliet, Mr. Brereton repeating those of Romeo, and Mr. Garrick, without hesitation, fixed on that character as a trial part for my *début*.

"It is impossible to describe the various emotions of hope and fear that possessed my mind when the important day was announced in the play-bills.

"The theatre was crowded with fashionable spectators: the green-room and orchestra (where Mr.

Garrick sat during the night) were thronged with critics. My dress was a pale pink satin, trimmed with crape, richly spangled with silver; my head was ornamented with white feathers, and my monumental suit, for the last scene, was white satin and completely plain; excepting that I wore a veil of the most transparent gauze, which fell quite to my feet from the back of my head, and a string of beads round my waist, to which was suspended a cross appropriately fashioned.

"When I approached the side wing my heart throbbed convulsively: I then began to fear that my resolution would fail, and I leaned upon the nurse's arm, almost fainting. Mr. Sheridan and several other friends encouraged me to proceed; and at length, with trembling limbs and fearful apprehension, I approached the audience.

"The thundering applause that greeted me nearly overpowered all my faculties. I stood mute and bending with alarm, which did not subside till I had feebly articulated the few sentences of the first short scene, during the whole of which I had never once ventured to look at the audience. On my return to the green-room, I was again encouraged, as far as my looks were deemed deserving of approbation; for of my powers nothing yet could be known, my fears having as it were palsied both my voice and action. The second scene being the masquerade, I had time to collect myself. I never shall forget the sensation which rushed through my bosom when I first looked towards the pit. I beheld a gradual ascent of heads: all eyes were fixed upon me; and the sensation they conveyed was awfully impressive: but the keen, the penetrating eyes of Mr. Garrick, darting their lustre from the centre of the orchestra, were, beyond all others, the objects most conspicuous.

"As I acquired courage I found the applause augment; and the night was concluded with peals of clamorous approbation. I was complimented on all sides; but the praise of one object, whom most I wished to please, was flattering even to the extent of human vanity. I then experienced, for the first time in my life, a gratification which language could not utter. I had till that period known no impulse beyond that of friendship; I had been an example of conjugal fidelity; but I had never known the perils to which the feeling heart is subjected, in an union of regard wholly uninfluenced by the affections of the soul.

"The second character which I played was Amanda, in 'A Trip to Scarbro.' The play was altered from Vanburgh's 'Relapse'; and the audience, supposing it was a new piece, on finding themselves deceived, expressed a considerable degree of disapprobation. I was terrified beyond imagination when Mrs. Yates, no longer able to bear the hissing of the audience, quitted the scene and left me alone to encounter the critic tempest. I stood for some moments as though I had been petrified: Mr. Sheridan, from the side wing, desired me not to quit the boards: the late Duke of Cumberland, from the stage-box, bade me take courage—'It is not you, but the play, they hiss,' said his Royal Highness. I curtsied; and that curtsey seemed to electrify the whole house; for a thundering peal of encouraging applause followed,—the comedy was suffered to go on, and is to this hour a stock play at Drury Lane Theatre.

"I often saw Mr. Sheridan, whose manner had lost nothing of its interesting attention. He continued to visit me very frequently, and always gave me the most friendly counsel. He knew that I was not properly protected by Mr. Robinson, but he was too generous to build his gratification on the detraction of another. The happiest moments I then knew were passed in the society of this distinguished being. He saw me ill-bestowed upon a man who neither loved nor valued me: he lamented my destiny, but with such delicate propriety, that it consoled while it revealed to me the unhappiness of my situation.

"My popularity increasing every night that I appeared, my prospects, both of fame and affluence, began to brighten. We now hired the house which is situated between the Hummums and the Bedford Arms, Covent Garden: it had been built (I believe) by Doctor Fisher, who married the widow of the celebrated actor Powell: but Mr. Robinson took the premises of Mrs. Mattocks, of Covent Garden Theatre. The house was particularly convenient in every respect; but, above all on account of its vicinity to Drury Lane. Here I hoped to enjoy, at least, some cheerful days, as I found that my circle of friends increased almost hourly. In proportion as play obtained its influence over my husband's mind, his small degree of remaining regard for me visibly decayed. We now had horses, a phaeton and ponies; and my fashions in dress were followed with flattering avidity. My house was thronged with visitors, and my morning levees were crowded, so that I could scarcely find a quiet hour for study. Mr. Sheridan was still my most esteemed of friends. He advised me with the gentlest anxiety, and he warned me of the danger which expense would produce, and which might interrupt the rising progress of my dramatic reputation. Situated as I was at this time, the effort was difficult to avoid the society of Mr. Sheridan. He was manager of the theatre. I could not shun seeing and conversing with him, at rehearsals and behind the scenes: and his conversation was always such as to fascinate and charm me. The green-room was frequented by nobility and men of genius; among these were Mr. Fox and the Earl of Derby. I had then been married more than four years, my daughter Maria Elizabeth nearly three years old. I had been then seen, and known, at all public places from the age of fifteen; yet I knew as little of the world's deceptions as though I had been educated in the deserts of Siberia. I believed every woman friendly, every man sincere, till I discovered proofs that their characters were deceptive.

"I had now performed two seasons, in tragedy and comedy. The play of THE WINTER'S TALE was this season commanded by their Majesties. I never had performed before the royal family; and the first character in which I was destined so to appear was that of PERDITA. I had frequently played the part, both with the Hermione of Mrs. Hartley and of Miss Farren; but I felt a strange degree of alarm when I found my name announced to perform it before the royal family.

"In the green-room I was rallied on the occasion; and Mr. Smith, whose gentlemanly manners and enlightened conversation rendered him an ornament to the profession, who performed the part of Leontes, laughingly exclaimed, 'By Jove, Mrs. Robinson, you will make a conquest of the Prince: for to-night you look handsomer than ever.' I smiled at the unmerited compliment; and little foresaw the vast variety of events that would arise from that night's exhibition!

"As I stood in the wing opposite the Prince's box, waiting to go on the stage, Mr. Ford, the manager's son, and now a respectable defender of the laws, presented a friend who accompanied him; this friend was Lord Viscount Malden, now Earl of Essex.

"We entered into conversation during a few minutes, the Prince of Wales all the time observing us, and frequently speaking to Colonel (now

General) Lake and to the Hon. Mr. Legge, brother to Lord Lewisham, who was in waiting on his Royal Highness. I hurried through the first scene, not without much embarrassment, owing to the fixed attention with which the Prince of Wales honoured me. Indeed, some flattering remarks which were made by his Royal Highness met my ear as I stood near his box, and I was overwhelmed with confusion.

"The Prince's particular attention was observed by every one, and I was again rallied at the end of the play. On the last curtsey, the royal family condescendingly returned a bow to the performers; but, just as the curtain was falling, my eyes met those of the Prince of Wales; and, with a look that I *never shall forget*, he gently inclined his head a second time: I felt the compliment, and blushed my gratitude.

"During the entertainment, Lord Malden never ceased conversing with me! he was young, pleasing, and perfectly accomplished. He remarked the particular applause which the Prince had bestowed on my performance, said a thousand civil things, and detained me in conversation till the evening's performance was concluded.

"I was now going to my chair, which waited,

when I met the royal family crossing the stage. I was again honoured with a very marked and low bow from the Prince of Wales. On my return home, I had a party to supper; and the whole conversation centred in encomiums on the person, graces, and amiable manners of the illustrious heir-apparent.

"Within two or three days of this time, Lord Malden made me a morning visit: Mr Robinson was not at home, and I received him rather awkwardly. But his Lordship's embarrassment far exceeded mine: he attempted to speak, paused, hesitated, apologized: I knew not why. He hoped I would pardon him; that I would not mention something he had to communicate; that I would consider the peculiar delicacy of his situation, and then act as I thought proper. I could not comprehend his meaning, and therefore requested that he would be explicit.

"After some moments of evident rumination, he tremblingly drew a small letter from his pocket. I took it, and knew not what to say. It was addressed to PERDITA. I smiled, I believe, rather sarcastically, and opened the *billet*. It contained only a few words, but those expressive of more than common civility: they were signed, FLORIZEL.

"'Well, my Lord, and what does this mean?' said I, half angry.

"'Can you not guess the writer?' said Lord Malden.

"'Perhaps yourself, my Lord?' cried I gravely.

"'Upon my honour, no,' said the Viscount. 'I should not have dared so to address you on so short an acquaintance.'

"I pressed him to tell me from whom the letter came. He again hesitated: he seemed confused and sorry that he had undertaken to deliver it. 'I hope that I shall not forfeit your good opinion,' said he, 'but——'

'But what, my Lord?'

"'I could not refuse,—for the letter is from the Prince of Wales.'

"I was astonished: I confess that I was agitated; but I was also somewhat sceptical as to the truth of Lord Malden's assertion. I returned a formal and a doubtful answer; and his Lordship shortly after took his leave.

"A thousand times did I read this short but expressive letter; still I did not implicitly believe that it was written by the Prince: I rather considered it as an experiment made by Lord Malden either on my vanity or propriety of conduct. On the next evening the Viscount repeated his visit: we had a card-party of six or seven, and the Prince of Wales was again the subject of unbounded panegyric. Lord Malden spoke of his Royal Highness's manners as the most polished and fascinating ; of his temper, as the most engaging ; and of his mind, the most replete with every amiable sentiment. I heard these praises, and my heart beat with conscious pride, while memory turned to the partial but delicately respectful letter which I had received on the preceding morning.

"The next day, Lord Malden brought me a second letter. He assured me that the Prince was most unhappy lest I should be offended at his conduct; and that he conjured me to go that night to the Oratorio, where he would by some signal convince me that he was the writer of the letters, supposing I was still sceptical as to their authenticity.

"I went to the Oratorio; and, on taking my seat in the balcony box, the Prince almost instantaneously observed me. He held the printed bill before his face, and drew his hand across his forehead ; still fixing his eyes on me. I was confused, and knew not what to do. My husband was with me, and I was fearful of his observing what passed. Still the Prince continued to make signs, such as moving his hand on the edge of the box as if writing, then speaking to the Duke of York (then Bishop of Osnaburg) who also looked towards me with particular attention.

" I now observed one of the gentlemen in waiting bring the Prince a glass of water: before he raised it to his lips, he looked at me. So marked was his Royal Highness's conduct that many of the audience observed it: several persons in the pit directed their gaze at the place where I sat; and, on the following day, one of the diurnal prints observed that there was one passage in Dryden's Ode which seemed particularly interesting to the Prince of Wales, who

'Gazed on the fair
Who caused his care,
And sigh'd, and look'd, and sigh'd again.'

" However flattering it might have been, to female vanity, to know that the most admired and most accomplished Prince in Europe was devotedly attached to me; however dangerous to the heart such idolatry as his Royal Highness, during many months, professed in almost daily letters, which were conveyed to me by Lord

Malden, still I declined any interview with his Royal Highness. I was not insensible to all his powers of attraction: I thought him one of the most amiable of men. There was a beautiful ingenuousness in his language, a warm and enthusiastic adoration expressed in every letter, which interested and charmed me. During the whole spring, till the theatre closed, this correspondence continued; every day giving me some new assurance of inviolable affection.

"After we had corresponded some months without ever speaking to each other (for I still declined meeting his Royal Highness, from a dread of the *éclat* which such a connection would produce, and the fear of injuring him in the opinion of his royal relatives) I received, through the hands of Lord Malden, the Prince's portrait in miniature painted by the late Mr. Meyer. This picture is now in my possession. Within the case was a small heart cut in paper, which I also have: on one side was written, '*Je ne change qu'en mourant.*' On the other, ' *Unalterable to my Perdita through life.*'

"During many months of confidential correspondence, I always offered his Royal Highness the best advice in my power; and disclaimed every sordid and interested thought. At every interview with Lord Malden, I perceived that he regretted the task he had undertaken; but he assured me that the Prince was almost frantic, whenever he suggested a wish to decline interfering. Once I remember his Lordship's telling me that the late Duke of Cumberland had made him a visit early in the morning, at his house in Clarges Street, informing him that the Prince was most wretched on my account, and imploring him to continue his services only a short time longer. The Prince's establishment was then in agitation: at this period his Royal Highness still resided in Buckingham House.

"A proposal was now made that I should meet his Royal Highness, at his apartments, in the disguise of male attire. I was accustomed to perform in that dress, and the Prince had seen me (I believe) in the character of the 'Irish Widow.' To this plan I decidedly objected. The indelicacy of such a step, as well as the danger of detection, made me shrink from the proposal. My refusal threw his Royal Highness into the most distressing agitation, as was expressed by the letter which I received on the following morning. Lord Malden again lamented that he had engaged himself in the intercourse; and declared that he had himself conceived so violent a passion for me that he was the most miserable and unfortunate of mortals.

"During this period, though Mr Robinson was a stranger to my epistolary intercourse with the Prince, his conduct was entirely neglectful. He was perfectly careless respecting my fame and my repose. His indifference naturally produced an alienation of esteem on my side, and the increasing adoration of the most enchanting of mortals hourly reconciled my mind to the idea of a separation. The unbounded assurances of lasting affection which I received from his Royal Highness in many scores of the most eloquent letters, the contempt which I experienced from my husband, and the perpetual labour which I underwent for his support, at length began to weary my fortitude. Still I was reluctant to become the theme of public animadversion; and still I remonstrated with my husband, on the unkindness of his conduct."

It should be mentioned that these candid confessions were written at a period when her frailties had been condoned and she had found a number of friends and acquaintances of a respectable character, who felt that a weak and interesting woman had been deliberately made the victim of one of the most selfish and unprincipled of men. The unfortunate lady was quite dazzled by the tinsel charms of this sham Adonis, and seemed to find something more than mortal in the florid beauty of this most gross and selfish of admirers. Without officially extenuating her follies, this much may be said, that she is entitled to some indulgence on the ground of the neglect of the husband who should have protected her, and the persevering arts that were employed to ensnare her. A still more favourable extenuation was, that being of an unformed and romantic turn, it was artfully attempted to give a sentimental and comparatively innocent turn to the affair, and incidents of secrecy, disguise, mufflings, &c., were employed by the precocious lover, who had dubbed himself Florizel, and the finished scoundrel, Lord Malden, who acted as his agent in the affair. The loves of Florizel and Perdita sounded prettily in the newspapers, which in the obsequious jargon then fashionable spoke of one " whose manners were resistless and whose was victory."

At length " after many alternations of feeling," a meeting was arranged under circumstances of the most melodramatic character.

"Lord Malden and myself dined at the inn on the island between Kew and Brentford. We waited the signal for crossing the river, in a boat which had been engaged for the purpose. Heaven can witness how many conflicts my agitated heart endured at this important moment! I admired the Prince; I felt grateful for his affection. *He was the most engaging of created beings.* I had corresponded with him during many months, and his eloquent letters, the exquisite sensibility which breathed through every line, his ardent professions of adoration, had combined to shake my feeble resolution. The handkerchief was waved on the opposite shore; but the signal was, by the dusk of the evening, rendered almost imperceptible. Lord Malden took my hand; I stepped into the boat, and in a few minutes we landed before the iron gates of old Kew Palace. The interview was but of a moment. The Prince of Wales and the Duke of York (then Bishop of Osnaburg) were walking down the avenue. They hastened to meet us. A few words, and those scarcely articulate, were uttered by the Prince, when a noise of people approaching from the palace startled us. The moon was now rising; and the idea of being overheard, or of his Royal Highness being seen out at so unusual an hour, terrified the whole group. After a few more words of the most affectionate nature uttered by the Prince, we parted, and Lord Malden and myself returned to the island. The Prince never quitted the avenue, nor the presence of the Duke of York, during the whole of this short meeting. Alas! my friend, if my mind was before influenced by esteem, it was now awakened to the most enthusiastic admiration. The rank of the Prince no longer chilled into awe that being, who now considered him as the lover and the friend. *The graces of his person, the irresistible sweetness of his smile, the tenderness of his melodious yet manly voice, will be remembered by me* till every vision of this changing scene shall be forgotten.

"Many and frequent were the interviews which afterwards took place at this romantic spot: our walks sometimes continued till past midnight; the Duke of York and Lord Malden were always of the party; our conversation was composed of general topics. The Prince had, from his infancy, been wholly secluded, and naturally took much pleasure in conversing about the busy world, its manners and pursuits, characters and scenery. Nothing could be more delightful or more rational than our midnight perambulations. I always wore a dark-coloured habit: the rest of our party generally wrapped themselves in great coats to disguise them, excepting the Duke of York, who almost universally alarmed us by the display of a buff coat, the most conspicuous colour he could have selected for an adventure of this nature. The polished and fascinating ingenuousness of his Royal Highness's manners contributed not a little to enliven our promenades. He sang with exquisite taste; and the tones of his voice breaking on the silence of the night, have often *appeared to my entranced senses like more than mortal melody.* Often have I lamented the distance which destiny had placed between us: how would my soul have idolized such a *husband!* Alas! how often, in the ardent enthusiasm of my soul, have I formed the wish that being were *mine alone!* to whom partial millions were to look up for protection.

"The Duke of York was now on the eve of quitting the country for Hanover: the Prince was also on the point of receiving his first establishment; and the apprehension that this attachment might injure his Royal Highness, in the opinion of the world, rendered the caution, which was invariably observed, of the utmost importance. A considerable time elapsed in these delightful scenes of visionary happiness. The Prince's attachment seemed to increase daily, and I considered myself as the most blest of human beings. During some time, we had enjoyed our meetings in the neighbourhood of Kew; and I now only looked forward to the adjusting of his Royal Highness's establishment for the public avowal of our mutual attachment.

"I had relinquished my profession. The last night of my appearance on the stage, I represented the character of Sir Harry Revel, in the comedy of 'The Miniature Picture,' written by Lady Craven;* and 'The Irish Widow.' On entering the green-room, I informed Mr. Moody, who played in the farce, that I should appear no more after that night; and, endeavouring to smile while I sang, I repeated,

'Oh joy to you all in full measure,
So wishes and prays Widow Brady!'

which were the last lines of my song in 'The Irish Widow.' This effort to conceal the emotion I felt, on quitting a profession I enthusiastically loved, was of short duration; and I burst into tears on my appearance. My regret, at recollecting that I was treading for the last time the boards

* Now Margravine of Anspach.

where I had so often received the most gratifying testimonies of the public approbation, where mental exertion had been emboldened by private worth, that I was flying from a happy certainty, perhaps to pursue the phantom disappointment, nearly overwhelmed my faculties, and for some time deprived me of the power of articulation. Fortunately, the person on the stage with me had had to begin the scene, which allowed me time to collect myself. I went, however, mechanically dull through the business of the evening; and, notwithstanding the cheering expressions and applause of the audience, I was several times near fainting.

"The daily prints now indulged the malice of my enemies by the most scandalous paragraphs respecting the Prince of Wales and myself. I found it was too late to stop the hourly augmenting torrent of abuse that was poured upon me from all quarters. Whenever I appeared in public, I was overwhelmed by the gazing of the multitude. I was frequently obliged to quit Ranelagh, owing to the crowd which staring curiosity had assembled round my box; and, even in the streets of the metropolis, I scarcely ventured to enter a shop without experiencing the greatest inconvenience. Many hours have I waited till the crowd dispersed which surrounded my carriage in expectation of my quitting the shop. I cannot suppress a smile at the absurdity of such proceeding, when I remember that, during nearly three seasons I was almost every night upon the stage, and that I had then been nearly five years with Mr. Robinson at every fashionable place of entertainment. But, thank Heaven! my heart was not formed in the mould of callous effrontery. I shuddered at the gulf before me, and felt small gratification in the knowledge of having taken a step which many, who condemned, would have been no less willing to imitate, had they been placed in the same situation."

In this sort of Della Cruscan dream the unfortunate lady was living, forming perspectives of yet more delightful visions beyond. But she did not know of what was a specially disagreeable feature in the character of one who was to be the future first gentleman in Europe. An almost invariable portion of his programme in such *affaires de cœur* was a sudden desertion, as abrupt as his advances had been gradual and impassioned. Full of anticipations the most romantic, and shutting her eyes to all consequences, the deceived lady had taken her leave of the stage.

"The period now approached that was to destroy all the fairy visions which had filled my mind with dreams of happiness. At the moment when everything was preparing for his Royal Highness's establishment, when I looked impatiently for the arrival of that day on which I might behold my adored friend gracefully receiving the acclamations of his future subjects, when I might enjoy the public protection of that being for whom I gave up all, I received a letter from his Royal Highness, a cold and unkind letter—briefly informing me that '*we must meet no more!*'

"And now, suffer me to call GOD to witness, that I was unconscious why this decision had taken place in his Highness's mind: only two days previous to this letter being written I had seen the Prince at Kew, and his affection appeared to be boundless as it was undiminished.

"Amazed, afflicted beyond the power of utterance, I wrote immediately to his Royal Highness and required an explanation. He remained silent. Again I wrote, but received no elucidation of this most cruel and extraordinary mystery. The Prince was then at Windsor. I set out in a small pony phæton, wretched, and unaccompanied by any one except my postillion (a child of nine years of age). It was nearly dark when we quitted Hyde Park Corner. On my arrival at Hounslow, the innkeeper informed me that every carriage which had passed the heath for the last ten nights had been attacked and rifled. I confess the idea of personal danger had no terrors for my mind, in the state it then was; and the possibility of annihilation, divested of the crime of suicide, encouraged rather than diminished my determination of proceeding. We had scarcely reached the middle of the heath when my horses were startled by the sudden appearance of a man, rushing from the side of the road. The boy on perceiving him instantly spurred his pony, and, by a sudden bound of our light vehicle, the ruffian missed his grasp at the front rein. We now proceeded at full speed, while the footpad ran, endeavouring to overtake us. At length, my horses fortunately outrunning the perseverance of the assailant, we, at last, reached the Magpie, a small inn on the heath, in safety. The alarm which, in spite of my resolution, this adventure had created, was augmented on my recollecting for the first time, that I had then in my black stock a brilliant stud of very considerable value, which could only have been possessed by the robber by strangling the wearer.

"If my heart palpitated with joy at my escape from assassination, a circumstance soon after occurred that did not tend to quiet my emotion. This was the appearance of Mr. H. Meynel and Mrs. A———. My foreboding soul instantly beheld a rival, and, with jealous eagerness, interpreted the hitherto inexplicable conduct of the Prince, from his having frequently expressed his wish to know that lady.

"On my arrival, the Prince would not see me. My agonies were now indescribable. I consulted with Lord Malden and the Duke of Dorset, whose honourable mind and truly disinterested friendship had, on many occasions, been exemplified towards me. They were both at a loss to divine any cause of this sudden change in the Prince's feelings. The Prince of Wales had hitherto assiduously sought opportunities to distinguish me more publicly than was prudent, in his Royal Highness's situation. This was in the month of August. On the fourth of the preceding June, I went, by his desire, into the Chamberlain's box at the birthnight ball: the distressing observation of the circle was drawn towards the part of the box in which I sat, by the marked and injudicious attentions of his Royal Highness. I had not been arrived many minutes before I witnessed a singular species of fashionable coquetry. Previous to his Highness's beginning his minuet, I perceived a woman of high rank select from the bouquet she wore, two rosebuds, which she gave to the Prince, as he afterwards informed me, 'emblematical of herself and him:' I observed his Royal Highness immediately beckon to a nobleman, who has since formed a part of his establishment, and, looking most earnestly at me, whisper a few words, at the same time presenting to him his newly acquired trophy. In a few moments Lord C. entered the Chamberlain's box, and giving the rosebuds into my hands, informed me that he was commissioned by the Prince to do so. I placed them in my bosom, and, I confess, felt proud of the power by which I thus publicly mortified an exalted rival. His Royal Highness now avowedly distinguished me at all public places of entertainment; at the King's hunt, near Windsor, at the reviews, and at the theatres. The Prince only seemed happy in evincing his affection towards me.

"How terrible then was the change to my feelings! And I again most SOLEMNLY REPEAT, that I was totally ignorant of any JUST CAUSE for so sudden an alteration.

"My 'good-natured friends' now carefully informed me of the multitude of secret enemies who were ever employed in estranging the Prince's mind from me. So fascinating, so illustrious a lover could not fail to excite the envy of my own sex. Women of all descriptions were emulous of attracting his Royal Highness's attention. Alas! I had neither rank nor power to oppose such adversaries. Every engine of female malice was set in motion to destroy my repose; and every petty calumny was repeated with tenfold embellishments. Tales of the most infamous and glaring falsehood were invented; and I was again assailed by pamphlets, by paragraphs, by caricatures, and all the artillery of slander, while the only being to whom I then looked up for protection was so situated as to be unable to afford it. In the anguish of my soul, I once more addressed the Prince of Wales. I complained, perhaps too vehemently, of his injustice; and of the calumnies which had been by my enemies fabricated against me, of the falsehood of which he was but too sensible. I conjured him to render me justice. He did so: he wrote me a most eloquent letter, disclaiming the causes alleged by a calumniating world, and fully acquitting me of the charges which had been propagated to destroy me.

"I resided now in Cork Street, Burlington Gardens. The house, which was neat, but by no means splendid, had recently been fitted up for the reception of the Countess of Derby, on her separation from her lord. My situation now every hour became more irksome. The Prince still unkindly persisted in withdrawing himself from my society. I was now deeply involved in debt, which I despaired of ever having the power to discharge. I had quitted both my husband and my profession;—the retrospect was dreadful!

"My estrangement from the Prince was now the theme of public animadversion, while the newly invigorated shafts of my old enemies, the daily prints, were again hurled upon my defenceless head, with tenfold fury. The regrets of Mr. Robinson, now that he had *lost* me, became insupportable;—he constantly wrote to me in the language of unbounded affection; nor did he fail, when we met, to express his agony at our separation, and even a wish for our re-union.

"I had, at one period, resolved on returning to my profession; but some friends whom I consulted dreaded that the public would not suffer my reappearance on the stage. This idea intimidated me, and precluded my efforts for that independence of which my romantic credulity had robbed me. I was fatally induced to relinquish what would have proved an ample and honourable resource for myself and my child. My debts accumulated to near seven thousand pounds. My creditors, whose insulting illiberality could only be equalled by their unbounded impositions, hourly assailed me.

"I was, in the meantime, wholly neglected by the Prince, while the assiduities of Lord Malden daily increased. I had no other friend on whom I could rely for assistance or protection. When I say protection, I would not be understood to mean *pecuniary* assistance—Lord Malden being, at the time alluded to, even poorer than myself: the death of his Lordship's grandmother, Lady Frances Coningsby, had not then placed him above the penury of his own small income.

"Lord Malden's attention to me again exposed him to all the humiliation of former periods. The Prince assured me once more of his wishes to renew our former friendship and affection, and urged me to meet him at the house of Lord Malden in Clarges Street. I was at this period little less than frantic, deeply involved in debt, persecuted by my enemies, and perpetually reproached by my relations. I would joyfully have resigned an existence now become to me an intolerable burthen; yet my pride was not less than my sorrow, and I resolved, whatever my heart might suffer, to wear a placid countenance when I met the inquiring glances of my triumphant enemies.

"After much hesitation, by the advice of Lord Malden, I consented to meet his Royal Highness. He accosted me with every appearance of tender attachment, declaring that he had never for one moment ceased to love me—but, that I had many concealed enemies, who were exerting every effort to undermine me. We passed some hours in the most friendly and delightful conversation, and I began to flatter myself that all our differences were adjusted. But what words can express my surprise and chagrin, when, on meeting his Royal Highness *the very next day* in Hyde Park, he turned his head to avoid seeing me, and even affected *not to know me!*

"Overwhelmed by this blow, my distress knew no limits. Yet Heaven can witness the truth of my assertion, even in this moment of complete despair, when oppression bowed me to the earth, I blamed not the Prince. I did then, and ever shall consider his mind as nobly and honourably organized! nor could I teach myself to believe that a heart, the seat of so many virtues, could possibly become inhuman and unjust."

There was some "secret history" connected with this affair, and it turned out that the sacrifice of the unhappy lady had been found profitable to the two parties which were then at war—the Court and the Prince. A reconciliation was effected, and the Prince was delighted to pay a cheap tribute to public decorum by resigning what he no longer cared to keep, and receiving as his reward that "establishment," and adjustment which had formed such a brilliant vista in the poor lady's dreams.*

Though the magnanimous Prince was to benefit so handsomely by his sacrifice, his intention apparently was that this disagreeable affair should be closed with the smallest expense conceivable. No answer was given to the lady's letters. She had abandoned her profession, and had been cast off by her husband. Fortunately she held a bond of her royal admirer's for twenty thousand pounds payable on his "establishment." All such august securities are of little value, save as instruments of negotiation and compromise—it being almost impossible to enforce their payment. Armed with

* See Letters of George the Third to Lord North.

this document, her friends now interfered, and after much discreditable haggling it was felt that some settlement could not be refused with decency. Mr. Fox undertook the office of arbitrator, and decided that the bond should be given up in consideration of an annuity of five hundred a year. Thus prosaically ended the history of Florizel and Perdita.

The rest of her life offered but little interest. The harsh treatment she had met with excited sympathy, and found her some friends of a reputable class. She was privileged to sustain the rôle of a heroine "that had suffered"—and, owing to a tone then fashionable in society and encouraged by the Press, awakened a fresh interest by becoming a disciple of the sentimental school of which Mr. Merry was chief professor. This taste was chiefly manifested in feeble verses—known as "Poems" —which were thrown off on any occasion that was suitably romantic. Thus it was rumoured in the papers that in the winter of 1790 "Mrs. Robinson had entered into a poetical correspondence with Mr. Robert Merry under the fictitious names of 'Laura' and 'Laura Maria'— Mr. Merry assuming the title of 'Della Crusca.'" One result of which graceful interchange of sentiment was a work described as "a quarto Poem"—and entitled 'Ainsi va le Monde.' It contained three hundred and fifty lines, yet it was "written in twelve hours, as a reply to Mr. Merry's '*Laurel of Liberty*,' which had been sent to Mrs. Robinson on a Saturday: on the Tuesday following the answer was composed and given to the public."—The subjects that inspired her muse illustrate very happily the character of the "sentiment" of that day which is scarcely intelligible to our own generation. In such soft communings the Sewards, Pratts, Hayleys, and others wasted many profitable hours, and much good ink.

The heroine did not, however, content herself with these *dilettante* exercises, and it is to be feared did not limit herself to the character of "a fair Platonist," as the newspapers of her day might have styled her. She repaired to foreign climes, where her rather frivolous nature was gratified by homage and attentions of a more doubtful kind.*

* Her biographer, approaching this part of her career, has delicately relegated to a note what really ought to have found an official place in a regular account of her life. And the passage is worth considering, as a specimen of that valet-like style in which it was then customary to dwell on the trespasses of the noble and the fashionable. "An attachment took place between Mrs. Robinson and Colonel Tarleton, shortly after the return of the latter from America, which subsisted

During the expedition thus alluded to she entirely lost the use of her limbs, and in spite of every remedy remained almost a cripple for the rest of her life. She was but twenty-four when this affliction befell her. She tried the baths of Aix-la-Chapelle, where, we are assured, "a dawn of comparative tranquillity soothed her spirits." Finding all these attempts useless, she resigned herself to what she was obliged to endure—and during the rest of her life devoted herself to what was called "literary labour," *i.e.*, to the composition of indescribably vapid " Poems " on her own blighted affections, on the death of her father and mother, and which her biographer moderately commends as "not worse than other effusions of the same class." A long course of ill health at last ended in disease and death. She wished to return to her birth-place, and die there, but even this sad solace was denied to her, from a want of the pecuniary means for its execution. In vain she applied to those on whom

during sixteen years. *On the circumstances which occasioned its dissolution, it is neither necessary, nor would it be proper to dwell.* The exertions of Mrs. Robinson in the service of Col. Tarleton, when pressed by pecuniary embarrassment, led to that unfortunate journey, the consequences of which proved so fatal to her health. The Colonel accompanied her to the Continent; and, by his affectionate attentions, sought to alleviate those sufferings of which he had been the involuntary occasion."

honour, humanity, and justice gave her undoubted claims. She even condescended to entreat, as a *donation*, the return of those sums granted as *a loan* in her prosperity.

"The following is a copy of a letter addressed, on this occasion, to a *noble* debtor, and found among the papers of Mrs. Robinson after her decease:—

"April 23, 1800.

"My Lord,—Pronounced by my physicians to be in a rapid decline, I trust that your Lordship will have the goodness to assist me with a part of the sum for which you are indebted to me. Without your aid I cannot make trial of the Bristol waters, the *only* remedy that presents to me any hope of preserving my existence. I should be sorry to *die* at enmity with any person; and you may be assured, my dear Lord, that I bear none towards you. It would be useless to ask you to call on me; but, if you would do me that honour, I should be happy, *very happy*, to see you, being,

"My dear Lord, yours truly,
"Mary Robinson."

To this letter no answer was returned! Further comments are unnecessary.

"Her disorder rapidly drawing towards a period,

the accumulation of water upon her chest every moment threatened suffocation. For nearly fifteen nights and days she was obliged to be supported upon pillows, or in the arms of her young and affectionate nurses. Her decease, through this period, was hourly expected. On the twenty-first of December, she inquired how near was Christmas Day. Being answered, Within a few days—' *Yet*,' said she, 'I shall never see it.' The remainder of this melancholy day passed in indescribable tortures. Towards midnight, the sufferer exclaimed, 'Oh God, oh just and merciful God, help me to support this agony!' The whole of the ensuing day she continued to endure great anguish. In the evening, a kind of lethargic stupor came on. Miss Robinson, approaching the pillow of her expiring mother, earnestly conjured her to speak if in her power. '*My darling Mary!*' she faintly articulated, and *spoke no more*. In another hour she became insensible to the grief of those by whom she was surrounded, and breathed her last at a quarter past twelve on the following noon."

Thus ended the career of this unhappy lady. In harmony with the cynical truth of the unnoticed appeal to the noble lord which was in keeping with the gracious manners of the Prince's Court, is Miss

Hawkins' unsparing sketch: "She was unquestionably very beautiful, but more so in the face than in the figure; and as she proceeded in her course she acquired a remarkable facility in adapting her deportment to her dress. When she was to be seen daily in St. James's Street or Pall Mall, even in her chariot, the variation was striking. To-day she was a *paysanne*, with her straw hat tied at the back of her head, looking as if too new to what she passed to know what she looked at. Yesterday, perhaps, she had been the dressed belle of Hyde Park, trimmed, powdered, patched, painted to the utmost power of rouge and white lead; to-morrow she would be the cravated Amazon of the riding-house; but be she what she might, the hats of the fashionable promenaders swept the ground as she passed. But in her outset 'the style' was a high phaeton, in which she was driven by the favoured of the day. Three candidates and her husband were outriders: and this in the face of the congregations turning out of places of worship. . . . . . . About the year 1778 she appeared on the stage, and gained, from the character in which she charmed, the name of *Perdita*. She then started in one of the new streets of Marylebone, and was in her altitude.

Afterwards, when a little in the wane, she resided under protection in Berkeley Square, and appeared to guests as mistress of the house as well as of its master. Her manners and conversation were said by those invited to want refinement. . . . . . I saw her on one day handed to her outrageously extravagant *vis-à-vis* by a man whom she pursued with a doting passion; all was still externally brilliant: she was fine and fashionable and the men of the day in Bond Street still pirouetted as her carriage passed them: the next day the vehicle was reclaimed by the maker; the Adonis whom she courted fled her: she followed—all to no purpose. She then took up a new life in London, became literary. . . . . . . What was the next glimpse? On a table in one of the waiting-rooms of the Opera House was seated a woman of fashionable appearance, still beautiful, 'but not in the bloom of beauty's pride;' she was not noticed except by the eye of pity. In a few minutes two liveried servants came to her, and they took from their pockets long white sleeves, which they drew on their arms; they then lifted her up and conveyed her to her carriage—it was the then helpless, paralytic *Perdita!*"

CHAPTER V.

GEORGE FREDERICK COOKE.

GEORGE FREDERICK COOKE,* in spite of all his rudeness and irregularities, is a figure on which the eye rests with a curious interest. There was an originality and piquancy in the various bursts of his extravagance which was quite dramatic, and diverting in the highest degree: so much so that the sober Cooke is almost uninteresting compared with his intoxicated self. In that condition he became grotesque, brutal, mock-heroic, and even witty— his sarcasm was withering, so that the victim of his humour was, from self-respect, compelled to deal with him as a sober being. Beside this odd reputation, his theatrical character seems comparatively tame and faded. There are grand traditions of his power and fierce energies in such parts as Richard and Sir Giles Overreach, and his genius seems to have been of the same surging and tempestuous quality as Edmund Kean's; but the peculiar features of his style do not stand out very distinctly.

* Born 1756—died 1812.

All the adventures and outbursts of "GEORGE FREDERICK COOKE"—for he and his friends delighted in the ring of these words, and would not have abated one of the three names—have a flavour of their own, and are still retailed with *goût* by old actors. There are stories of his quarrelsomeness, of his sardonic raillery when in his cups, and, above all, of his moody jealousy against what he considered the "priggish" superiority of Kemble, whom he considered his inferior in genius, though more artful and and decorous. On these grounds, therefore, because he was a thoroughly genuine character, recklessly sacrificing himself sooner than pay the homage usually offered by irregularity to decency, he really stands apart from the rest of his profession, a Bohemian as it is called, and a not unpicturesque figure.

This bitterness, combined with a haughtiness worthy of a Spanish hidalgo, might have received some indulgence, as it seems to have been founded on a sense of humiliation and the consciousness that his infirmities had placed him below men to whom he was superior. He always appeared to feel that he had committed his reputation, and could not hope to retrieve himself: and therefore took refuge in a quarrelsome sensitiveness, which was yet not without dignity. A history might almost be written of his strange freaks of drunkenness, and in such a record a special study of the humours of George Frederick Cooke would have to be made. The sudden turn from good-nature and affection to hostility was the most familiar shape of his humour: and in this mood he may be most characteristically introduced.

"Mr. Cooper, the American tragedian," says Mr. Mathews, "had been performing a series of characters at Drury Lane Theatre; and being extremely intimate with Cooke, it occurred to him that his performance with him in 'Othello' on his benefit night would be a great attraction, if Mr. Harris's permission could be obtained. Cooke, who, in his natural character, was one of the kindest of men, instantly undertook to apply to Mr. Harris, giving Cooper some hope of success.

"Mr. Harris resided at this period at Belmont, near Uxbridge, where one afternoon Mr. Cooke was announced. The weather was intensely severe, and the visit augured some pressing cause; for Cooke seldom called but to make some request, generally difficult to be reconciled or granted. Still on the present occasion, Mr. Harris was 'very happy to see Mr. Cooke,' and 'hoped he came to stay dinner;' which hope was unnoticed by the actor, who nervously proceeded to break the unreasonable nature of his visit, and he began in broken accents to explain his errand: 'My *dear* sir!—Cooper—the best creature in the world—been acting at Drury Lane—going to take a benefit—Othello—Iago—bring him a great house. In fine, *would* Mr. Harris allow him (Cooke) to perform the character of Iago for his friend on his benefit night?'

"Mr. Harris looked very blank at this certainly unfair demand upon his self-interest. He shook his head ominously, and gravely asked Mr. Cooke whether he did not think it *rather* more than he ought to grant, considering the vast importance of his exclusive services. These and other arguments were mildly but determinately combated by Cooke in his best and most gentlemanlike manner; for 'Cooper, the best creature in the world,' was to be served; and Mr. Harris being at length overcome, Cooke's heart and eyes overflowed with generous delight and gratitude for the power thus afforded him to benefit a friend. Mr. Harris now reminded him of the dinner; but Cooke declined the invitation. 'No—he would take a crust, and one glass of wine to warm him, and then return to town.' After a polite struggle, Mr. Harris yielded to his visitor's determination; and a tray was produced, accompanied by a bottle of Madeira. Of this Cooke sipped and sipped with the most imperturbable self-complacency, until he nearly finished the bottle; when, by his master's order, the butler brought in another, of which Cooke had swallowed a few glasses, when a sudden recollection operated upon his mind, as Mr. Harris made some remark upon the increasing severity of the weather. Cooke a little '*warmed*' by the wine he had taken, now bethought himself of a circumstance which his fervour for his friend's interest and the Madeira had together totally obliterated for the time, for he arose abruptly, and taking Mr. Harris's hand, broke to him this new matter: 'My *dear sir*, your goodness so overpowered all other recollections, that it made me entirely forget that I left my friend, dear Cooper, the best creature in the world, at the gate when I came in. Let me send for him, to thank you for your generous permission in his favour.'

"Mr. Harris was in much distress, and in spite of Cooke's assuring him that 'dear Cooper' would not mind it, he being 'the best creature in the world,' rang the bell, and desired the servant to request Mr. Cooper's company within doors. By this time the Madeira might be said to have *warmed* Mr. Cooke more than half through ; the second bottle was rapidly diminishing, and he was full of feelings generous as the wine. Again and again he clasped his liberal manager's hands in thankfulness for his kindness, reiterating, ' My *dear sir*, you're *too good* to me! I can never repay such friendly treatment; I'm bound to you eternally.' &c. &c.

" Mr. Harris apologized to Mr. Cooper, and explained the cause of his tardy invitation, placing a chair for him near the fire. Cooke, without noticing him, continued his maudlin praise of his host's hospitality and goodness; afterwards informing Cooper of his having given consent to the performance in question; for which favour Mr. Cooper also expressed, as well as his shivering state would permit, his thanks, and, at the recommendation of Mr. Harris, accepted a glass of Madeira, in order to thaw his congealed faculties. Cooke was now all hilarity and happiness. Another bottle was suggested, and promptly supplied; and immediately the servant returned to announce the dinner, to which Mr. Harris again pressed Cooke and invited

Cooper. Mr. Cooke, however, would not hear of it. He *must*, he said, return to town to dinner, and 'dear Cooper' *must* accompany him ; and he insisted upon Mr. Harris leaving him and the 'best creature in the world' together in the library, where they would take 'just *one* glass more, and then depart.' During dinner, Mr. Harris related the occasion of Mr. Cooke's visit ; and in the course of the time, happened to inquire of the servants whether the gentlemen were gone. He was answered in the negative, and informed that Mr. Cooke had called for more wine, and that Mr. Cooper had vainly pressed him to depart. At this moment, a guest inquired whether Mr. Cooke performed that night, which question made Mr. Harris start from his chair in sudden alarm, exclaiming, 'Is this Wednesday? He *does* play ! What is it o'clock ?' at the same time taking out his watch in great agitation, he exclaimed, 'Take away the wine ; don't let him drink *a drop* more ! He must go away *directly*, or I shall have the theatre pulled down. He is advertised for " Richard the Third," and he can barely get back in time to dress ! '

"Back rushed the agitated proprietor to the library, where he found Cooper using every argument in his power to dissuade his indiscreet friend from drinking any more. But Cooke had already put too much of the enemy into his mouth not to be completely minus of brains, and, as usual under such privation, was utterly irrational and impersuasible.

"'Do you forget,' urged the unfortunate proprietor, 'that this is a play-night, Mr. Cooke? Even now you are expected in town. I entreat you will go without further delay, or you will be too late.'

"Cooke, in what he meant to be a most insinuating tone of voice, *blessed* his 'excellent friend;' again lauded his liberality and kindness, which he declared could never be forgotten or repaid by the devotion of his whole life, and finally begged the additional favour of *one* more bottle of his Madeira for himself and 'dear Cooper,' who, he repeated for the twentieth time, was 'the best creature in the world.' To this request Mr. Harris gave a positive and concise negative, placing before Mr. Cooke's view the danger he was hazarding by delay, and rendering himself unfit for his evening's duty. All was in vain; for Cooke, though equally civil, was also determined, and again and again coaxingly urged his request for *one* more bottle.

At length, finding Mr. Harris inflexible, the Madeira he *had* drunk began to proclaim the indignation it had engendered in Mr. Cooke's grateful bosom; and as the liquor fermented, it raised the recipient up to a state of inflation which threatened to burst all bounds, and he now assailed his host with the most opprobrious epithets; so that, eventually, by the potency of 'the drink,' his late 'excellent friend,' Mr. Harris, was converted into a 'vulgar, old, soap-boiling scoundrel,' who did not know how to treat a *gentleman* when one condescended to visit him; and Mr. Harris was imperiously asked, '*Do you know who I am, sir? Am I not George Frederick Cooke?*—without whose talents you would be confined to your own grease-tub; and who will never more darken your inhospitable doors while he lives, nor uphold your contemptible theatre any longer after this night!' And with many other threats and delicate inuendoes in relation to Mr. Harris's soap-boiling pursuits not herein set down, he staggered out of the room with the assistance of the 'best creature in the world,' whom he now distinguished by every ill name that drunkenness could remember or invent, for daring to direct or control *him*, *George Frederick Cooke!* when the great tragedian reeled into the attendant chaise, and was driven to town with his grieved and much-abused friend, 'dear Cooper!'

"That night the audience did *not* mistake 'the drunkard for a god,' for the great 'George Frederick Cooke' was hissed off the stage, and obliged to leave his performance unfinished; and it was some time ere 'Richard was himself again.'"

The result of such afternoon excesses was that most degrading of all spectacles, the exhibition of an actor on the stage, who is scarcely able to articulate or indeed to support himself. The curious contrast between what a vast audience comes to witness—intellect in its highest and most finished development, and what *is* presented, viz. intellect in its lowest and most bestial condition, produces a sort of surprise and disgust which is almost dramatic. The ordinary victims of this failing may at least shrink from the public gaze, but it is an additional penalty for the actor of talent who is thus afflicted that, in spite of all his efforts his halting figure, his thick and rambling speeches must betray to the crowd that he is unfit to appear before them, and that he is only insulting them by his incoherent attempts. Silence and perhaps pity may accept such lapses, but presently comes indignation, contempt and open jeering: while the less reputable part of the audience welcomes the exhibition as the most amusing part of the performance. What a picture of degradation is conveyed by the following scene:—

On one occasion, having vainly attempted to recall the beginning of Richard's first speech, he tottered forward with a cunning and maudlin intent to divert the resentment of the audience into a false channel: and laying his hand impressively upon his chest to insinuate that illness was the only cause of his failure, he with upturned mournful eyes solicited the sympathies of his audience and hiccupped out—"My old complaint!" A storm of hisses mingled with derisive merriment drove him off the stage.

Yet, as it must be owned, there was always a certain tragic dignity about his fits, which almost awed. Thus when he had been staggering about the Liverpool stage, scarcely able to articulate, a burst of hisses restored him to some coherence. He turned at bay and awed them with his fierce eyes.

"What! do you hiss me—*me*, George Frederick Cooke? *You contemptible money-getters.* You shall never again have *the honour* of hissing me! Farewell, I banish *you*. Then after a pause added, "*There's not a brick in your dirty town but what is cemented by the blood of a negro.*" They were cowed by this savage rebuke, and it must be said there is a certain rude grandeur in the rebuke. There is another scene that is really piquant, which exhibits him in his most characteristic mood.— He had been invited by a theatrical architect to dine, who was at a loss for a suitable person to invite to meet him. At last he pitched upon Mr. Brandon, the well-known manager of the front of the house at Covent Garden. The party was pleasant, but as usual Mr. Cooke began to drink deep, and gave promise of sitting on until far into the morning. The host, anxious to be rid of him before his dangerous mood came, dismissed him in plain terms, and took a candle to light him downstairs. When they were at the door the tragedian, who had accepted his *congé* in silence, suddenly seized his host *by his ears*, and shouted disdainfully, " Have I, George Frederick Cooke, degraded myself by dining *with bricklayers* to meet box-keepers!" and flinging him to the ground took his departure.

This strange being had married a lady of the name of Miss Daniells, and, it may be conceived, the lady led a troubled life. It was natural that his drunken humours, as regards her, should take the shape of ferocious jealousy, under which influence he at last locked her up in a high garret, and, taking the key with him, went off on one of his long debauches. He forgot all about her, and the poor woman was nearly starved. Her cries at last attracted the attention of the street, and she was released by means of a ladder. On this treatment she procured a separation.

There is another story also significant of that almost ferocious character which, as it were, lay concealed behind his nature until called into being by drink. When drinking at some low tavern he had got into a quarrel with a soldier, and insisted that his antagonist should fight him. The fellow made some excuses—among others that Cooke was a rich man, and had the advantage of him. Cooke pulled out a bundle of notes from his pocket, flung them on the fire, and kept them there with the poker until consumed; and, after they were consumed, said, "There goes every penny I have in the world. Now, sir, you *shall* fight me!"

The late Mr. Mathews used to describe an amusing evening which, when a beginner, he was privileged to spend with the great tragedian. The latter invited the novice into his room to supper. This was irresistible; and the invitation was promptly accepted.

"During the early part of the night the host was a most charming companion. He feelingly entered into the young man's (Charles Mathews) embarrassing situation, and offered to frank him home if he would consent to return to his respectable family, and give up the uncertain result of the trial he was making as an actor, but without any effect upon the aspiring candidate for dramatic fame.

"After supper, whisky punch, which was a novelty to Cooke, who had never before been in Ireland, was introduced, and he evidently was quite fascinated with the pleasing beverage. He grew gradually more animated in its praise; declared, as he sipped and sipped, that there was nothing like it! it was the nectar of the gods! His spirits increased in animation; and jug after jug was brought in. The young man had very early cried, 'Hold! enough!' Cooke, however, knew not satiety when once the brimming cup had been emptied. Mrs. Byrne, the landlady, up to a certain time, felt bound, both by duty and interest, to supply her distinguished lodger with what he called for; but at last, the night growing old, and her eyes not growing young, she felt disposed to give them rest; and, entering with the sixth jug, inquired respectfully, 'whether Mister Cooke would want anything more?' At this moment her lodger was warmed up into the most contented of beings. He glanced at the capacious vessel just replaced upon his table, and, believing its contents sufficient, exclaimed, 'Nothing more, my *good* Mrs. Byrne, nothing more.' Mrs. Byrne wished her two lodgers a good night, and retired. Cooke refilled his glass, and being somewhat sentimental, advised—admonished his young friend; above all, cautioned him to be industrious in his profession, sober in private, and not to allow company,—'villainous company,'—to be the ruin of his youth. And thus he lectured on sobriety, till glass after glass vanished, and with it the reality of the virtue he so eloquently recommended. At last the jug was again empty. Mr. Mathews rose to go. 'You shan't stir; we'll have another *croosken lawn*, my dear fellow, and then you shall go to bed. I have much more to say to you, my good boy. Sit down. You don't know me. The world don't know me. Many an hour that they suppose I have wasted in drinking, I have devoted to the study of my profession;—the Passions, and all their variations; their nice and imperceptible gradations. You shall see me delineate the Passions of the human mind.'

"The power of the whisky punch, however, acted in diametric opposition to the intent on his strong and flexible features, and only produced contortions and distortions, of which he was unconscious. He, nevertheless, endeavoured to illustrate the passions, while his visitor was to guess them. 'What's the meaning of that, eh?' said the tragedian, with a most inexplicable twist of his face. 'Sir!' said the timid spectator, puzzled what to call it. Cook reiterated 'What's the meaning of *that*? What passion does it express? Does it not strike you at once? There! What's that?' While he to whom he appealed could only say, '*Very fine*, sir!'—'But,' persisted Cooke, 'what *is* it?' He was then answered, 'Oh! I see, sir; *Anger!* to be sure!'—'To be sure you're a blockhead!' said Cooke, showing him the genuine expression of what he imputed to him before. 'Fear, sir! it was *Fear!* Now, then—what is *that?*'—'Oh, sir, *that*, I think, is meant for *Jealousy*.' Again the *passionate* man declared that the *guesser* was wrong. '*Jealousy!* Pooh, man! *Sympathy!* You're very dull, sir.—Now I will express a passion that you *can't* mistake. There! what's that? Look again, sir!' he exclaimed, in a terrific voice; and he then made up a hideous face, compounded of malignity and the leering of a drunken satyr, which he *insisted* upon being guessed; and his visitor, trembling for the consequences of another mistake, hesitatingly pronounced it to be, '*Revenge!*'— 'Despite o'erwhelm thee!' cried Cooke, in his most tragic rage. 'Revenge! Curse your stupidity! That was *Love!* Love, you insensible idiot! Can't you see it is Love?' Here he attempted the same expression, in order to strike conviction of its truth; when a mixture of comicality with the first effect so surprised the risible muscles of the young man, that he laughed outright. This infuriated the delineator of the Passions almost to madness. 'What, sir! does it make you laugh? Am I not George Frederick Cooke? born to command ten thousand slaves like thee! while you'll never get salt to your porridge, as an actor. *Who am I, sir?*'—curving his arms just as if preparing to make a minuet bow (his well-known attitude when *dignified*).

"'I beg your pardon, sir; the whisky punch has stupefied me.' Cooke accepted the excuse. 'True, true, *'tis out*' (his guest wished he was out too). 'Mistress Byrne, my love, another jug!' At this his companion made an attempt to go away, when he was forcibly dragged back with 'Stir not, on your life! The man that stirs makes me his foe. Another jug, sweet Mrs. Byrne!' Mrs. Byrne, it appeared, slept in the room under which this scene occurred; so that whenever Mr. Cooke addressed her he looked down upon the floor, as if more certain of his wishes reaching her, at the same time tapping with his foot.

"'Mistress Byrne, my darling, another jug, *sweet* Mrs. Byrne!' which she answered in tones quite audible through the slightly-built ceiling.

"'Indeed, Mr. Cooke, and I'm gone to bed, sure, and you can't have any more to-night.'

" *Cooke* (breaking the jug over her head).—' Do you hear *that*, Mistress Byrne?'

" *Mrs. B.*—'Indeed and I do, Mr. Cooke, sure enough!'

" *Cooke* (throwing in turns chairs, poker, tongs, and shovel down with a clash).—'Do you hear *that*, Mistress Byrne?'

"*Mrs. B.*—'God knows and I do, Mr. Cooke.'

"Mr. Cooke then began to throw the fragments he had made out of the window. The young man, apprehensive lest he might force him to make his exit after the damaged furniture, made another bold attempt to decamp. 'Stay where you are,' roared the now frenzied Cooke, grasping him violently. 'I will go,' said the now determined youth. 'Will you?' said Cooke. He then dragged his victim to the window, and roared out, 'Watch! Watch!' A watchman, who had been already attracted by the clatter amongst the movables, asked the cause of the disturbance; when, to the horror of his struggling prisoner, Cooke exclaimed, 'I give this man in charge; he has committed a capital offence—he has committed a murder.' 'I!' said his amazed companion. 'Yes,' said Cooke to the watchman, 'to my certain knowledge he has been this night guilty of a cruel, atrocious murder in cold blood. He has most barbarously murdered an inoffensive Jew-gentleman, of the name of *Mordeana*, and I charge him with it in the name of Macklin, author of "Love à la Mode."'. At this moment the supposed criminal slipped out of his grasp, and made for the door. Cooke followed him, and taking up the candles ran on the staircase with them, crying out, as he threw them and the candlesticks after him, ' Well, if you will go, you shan't say I sent you to bed without light !' But the young man reached his room, and, securely fastened in, he heard a long colloquy between the watchman and the tragedian, who had some trouble in explaining away the account he had given to him of the *murdered* ' Jew-gentleman.' "

But the story of his wild escapades darkens after his strange elopement to America in 1810, where he crowded into the space of a few weeks more violent eccentricity than he had ever exhibited during many years of his extravagant life. He was at the time engaged at Covent Garden, and the mysterious manner in which he was, as it were, smuggled out of England, with nightly journeyings in post chaises, secret embarkation, &c., was highly melodramatic. The real cause of the mystery was the uncertain humour of this singular being, whose nearest approach to a rational mood was a sort of gloomy torpor in the interval between his debauches. The rude fare and hardships of the voyage had the best effect on his health, and he arrived in the country, which he was destined never to leave, comparatively a new man.

His appearance at New York attracted what was considered the greatest house ever known in America. The effect of his great acting was prodigious. But after a few nights he began to yield to his old habits.

"During the time that had elapsed since his landing, Mr. Cooke had been gradually giving way more and more to his old enemy. His want of self-restraint had rendered it necessary to cease those invitations to dinner-parties which curiosity, and a desire to distinguish his talents, would otherwise have made incessant. But every night after acting was devoted to indulgence, and the consequent deplorable state sometimes extended to depriving him of voice on the following night of playing; but heretofore he had not exposed himself palpably to the public.

"After playing Sir Giles, he indulged himself as usual, but became unusually offensive in words and manner, as his unhappy madness increased; and at length, at variance with himself and his host, he retired sullenly to his chamber, and, as was frequent with him, sat up all night. In the morning, he went to bed. About noon he arose and leaving an excuse with the servant for not dining at home, went out without having seen any other part of the family.

"He rambled about the suburbs of the city in his solitary manner, for some hours, and then directed his steps to the Tontine Coffee House, the place at which he lodged upon his landing. Here he dined, and repeated his maddening draughts, till late at night, or in the morning, he again sunk to rest; if sinking to partial oblivion, overwhelmed by intemperance, deserves that quiet appellation. . . .

"The 19th December had been appointed for his benefit. 'Cato' was the play. The bills announced the last night of Mr. Cooke's engagement previous to his proceeding to Boston; the tragedy of 'Cato' and the farce of 'Love à la Mode,' for Mr. Cooke's benefit. The rehearsals of 'Cato' had been called, but the tragedy of 'Cato' was rehearsed without the presence of the hero. Cooke looked into the theatre on his way from the Coffee House to the manager's, and asked the prompter if 'all was well.' His appearance indicated too strongly that all was not well with him. He came into the green-room, and hearing the callboy call, as usual, the performers to come to the stage, by the names of the characters they were to represent—Juba — Syphax — Cato — he beckoned the boy to him.

"'My good lad, don't you know it's a benefit? we'll rehearse the play to-night.' . . .

"He then proceeded with the intent of removing his trunks to the Coffee House. Fortunately for him, a friend prevented him from carrying this design into execution, and upon being assured that no notice would be taken of his conduct, he gladly relinquished his plan, and dismissed the images of resentful enmity which he had conjured up to stimulate him to the act.

"In the meantime he had never read a line of Cato, and he was now incapable of reading to any purpose. The house filled. An audience so numerous, or more genteel, had never graced the walls of the New York theatre. The money received was eighteen hundred and seventy-eight dollars.

"Soon, very soon, it was perceived that the Roman patriot, the godlike Cato, was not to be seen in Mr. Cooke. The mind of the actor was utterly bewildered; he hesitated, repeated substituted speeches from other plays, or endeavoured to substitute incoherencies of his own—but his playing extempore was not so amusing as Sir

John's—the audience which had assembled to admire, turned away with disgust.

"After the play, I walked into the green-room. He was dressed for Sir Archy M'Sarcasm. As soon as he saw me, he came up to meet me, and exclaimed, ' Ah, it's all over now, we are reconciled—but I was very wild in the play—quite bewildered—do you know that I could not remember one line, after having recited the other—I caught myself once or twice giving Shakespeare for Addison;' and then with his chuckle and his eyes turned away, ' Heaven forgive me!—If you have ever heard anything of me, you must have heard that I always have a frolic on my benefit day. If a man cannot take a liberty with his *friends*, who the devil can he take a liberty with?'

"By the time the curtain drew up for the farce, he was so far recovered, that the words, being perfectly familiar, came trippingly from the tongue, and he being encouraged by finding himself in possession of his powers again, exerted them to the utmost, and played Sir Archy as well as ever he had done.

"He had played in New York seventeen nights, and the amount of money received by the manager was *twenty-one thousand five hundred and seventy-*

eight dollars. Making an average of $1269\frac{28}{100}$ dollars for each night.

"I had been told frequently of his asserting over the bottle, or under its influence, that he had been in America during our revolutionary contest, naming particularly the regiment he belonged to, speaking of various actions in which he had fought for his royal master, and discomfited and slaughtered the rebels; particularly one day when walking on our beautiful promenade, 'the battery,' and viewing the objects which adorn and surround one of the finest bays in the world, he called Mr. Price's attention to the heights of Brooklyn, and pointing, exclaimed:

"'That's the spot! *we* marched up! the rebels retreated! we charged! they fled! we mounted that hill—I carried the colours of the 5th, my father carried them before me, and my son now carries them—I led—Washington was in the rear of the rebels—I pressed forward—when at this moment, Sir William Howe, now Lord Howe, and the Lord for ever d—n him for it, cried halt!—but for that, sir, I should have taken Washington, and there would have been an end to the rebellion!'

"Notwithstanding his frequent recurrence to these rhodomontades, I had never heard him, until the day he embarked for Rhode Island, on his way to Boston, say anything which approached the subject. This morning in Broadway, on his road to the packet, he exclaimed, 'This is Broadway! This is the street through which Sir Henry Clinton used to gallop every day, full tilt! helter skelter! and his aids after him, as if the cry was, the devil take the hindmost!'

"I could not but be struck by this description of what I had so often seen when a boy; and though Mr. Cooke might have had this circumstance from various sources, he spoke so much like one describing what he had seen, that an impression was made upon my mind which the twenty months' hiatus in his chronicle revived in a very forcible manner.

"On the 6th he played Pierre to 368 dollars. This was a falling off indeed. He was next advertised for the favourite Sir Pertinax, but in vain; the amount was only 457 dollars on the 8th.

"That this failure of attraction sank deep into his wounded spirit, I had an opportunity afterwards of knowing. Of fortitude he had none: he sought oblivion in madness. . . .

"About ten o'clock in the morning of the 19th of February, 1811, after one of the most inclement nights of one of the coldest of our winters, when our streets were choked with ice and snow, a little girl came to the manager's office at the theatre with a note scarcely legible, running thus:

"'Dear Dunlap, send me one hundred dollars. G. F. COOKE.'

"I asked the child of whom she got the paper she had given me.

"'Of the gentleman, sir.'

"'Where is he?'

"'At our house.'

"'Where is that?'

"'In Reed Street, behind the Hospital.'

"'When did this gentleman come to your house?'

"'Last night, sir, almost morning—mother is sick sir, and I was sitting up with her, and a negro and a watchman brought the gentleman to our house and knocked, and we knew the watchman; and so mother let the gentleman come in and sit by the fire. He didn't want to come in at first, but said when he was at the door, "Let me lay down here and die."'

"Mr. Price came to the theatre, and I learned from him that Cooke having sat up late and become turbulent, to the annoyance of the family, he had insisted upon his going to bed, and he had apparently complied; but that when the household were all at rest, he had come down from his chamber, unlocked the street-door, and sallied out in the face of a west wind of more than Russian coldness. After consulting with Mr. Price, and showing the paper brought by the girl, I put one hundred dollars in small bank-notes in my pocket, and taking the messenger as my pilot, went in quest of George Frederick.

"As we walked, I asked my conductress what the gentleman had been doing since he came to her mother's house.

"'Sitting by the fire, sir, and talking.'

"'Has he had anything to drink?'

"'Yes, sir; he sent the negro man out for brandy, and he brought two quarts.—Poor old gentleman,' she continued, 'the people at the house where he lived must have used him very ill, and it was very cruel to turn him out o' doors *such a night.*'

"'Does he say he was turned out o' doors?'

"'Yes, sir,—he talks a great deal—to be sure I believe he is crazy.'

"We entered a small wooden building in Reed Street. The room was dark, and appeared the more so, owing to the transition from the glare of snow in the street. I saw nothing distinctly for the first moment, and only perceived that the place was full of people. I soon found that they were the neighbours, brought in to gaze at the strange, crazy gentleman: and the sheriff's officers distraining for the rent on the furniture of the sick widow who occupied the house.

"The bed of the sick woman filled one corner of the room, surrounded by curtains—sheriff's officers, a table, with pen, ink, and inventory, occupied another portion—a motley group, of whom Cooke was one, hid the fire-place from view, and the remainder of the apartment was filled by cartmen, watchmen, women, and children.

"When I recognised Cooke, he had turned from the fire, and his eye was on me with an expression of shame and chagrin at being found in such a situation. His skin and eyes were red, his linen dirty, his hair wildly pointing in every direction from his 'distracted globe,' and over his knee was spread an infant's bib, or something else, with which, having lost his pocket handkerchief, he wiped his incessantly moistened visage. After a wild stare at me, he changed from the first expression of his countenance, and welcomed me. He asked me why I had come. I replied, that I had received his note, and brought him the money he had required. I sat down by him, and after a few incoherent sentences of complaint, and entreaty that I would not leave him, he burst into tears. I soothed him and replied to his repeated entreaties of 'don't leave me,' by promises of remaining with him, but told him we must leave that place. He agreed, but added, with vehemence, 'Not back to his house! No, never! never!!'—Which apparent resolution he confirmed with vehement and reiterated oaths. The officer let me know that the gentleman had stopped the levying on the goods, and agreed to pay the quarter's rent. I was proceeding to make some inquiries, but Cooke, in the most peremptory tone, required that the money should be paid; as if fearing that his ability to fulfil his promise should be doubted by the bystanders. I paid the money and demanded a receipt. The officer, who was nearly drunk, asked for the gentleman's Christian name; when with all the dignity of the buskin the drooping hero raised his head, and roared out most discordantly, 'George Frederick! George Frederick Cooke!' The peculiar sharpness of the higher tones of his voice, joined to the unmelodious and croaking notes of debauchery, with his assumed dignity and squalid appearance, were truly comic though pitiable. . . .

"The next day after our arrival at Philadelphia, Mr. Cooke rehearsed Richard.

"After the rehearsal, he went to walk with the managers and see the city, while I attended to other engagements, having promised to meet him at Mr. Wood's, where we were to dine by invitation.

"We accordingly met and dined at Mr. Wood's, and I saw realised all that insanity of conduct, and licentiousness of speech, of which I had before heard much, but had never yet seen an exhibition.

"The party was principally theatrical, and after dinner, unfortunately the wine circulated more freely than the wit. My hero, who had protested in the morning that he would take care of himself, and only drink wine and water, was supplied by the politeness of his host with some good old port, which he threw down without remorse; but I cannot say without shame, for his eye most assiduously avoided mine, which probably he perceived had an expression of anxious watchfulness in it. The afternoon was oppressively warm, and seeing that Cooke's fate for the day was fixed, I retired to the house of a friend and took tea.

"Between eight and nine o'clock I returned to Mr. Wood's, and before I entered the door heard the high and discordant notes of George Frederick's voice. I found the party increased by the addition of some New York and Philadelphia gentlemen, who had been dining together elsewhere, and knowing that the veteran bacchanalian was here, called in to see him. And they saw an exhibition of him, in all the eccentricity of madness. Mr. Wood, whose habits were those of temperance, and whose health was delicate, had, according to a custom 'more honoured in the breach than the observance,' pushed about the bottle, and tasted to prove that it was good ; and was now primed with mirth, and so charged with words, that they flowed, or rather were thrown out, high, noisy, and foaming like the incessant stream of a *jet d'eau*. Cooke, infinitely annoyed at this never-ceasing eloquence from a Yankee manager, at a time too when he felt that all should attend to him, would interrupt his host by striking his fist on the table, and crying out with a tremendous shout, 'Hear me, sir!'

"When I came in he immediately made way for me near him, exclaiming, 'Ah! I see I was mistaken. I have been telling them that you were in bed by this time ; but I see how it is, you have been taking your tea. He owns himself to be a tea-sot. He is the only man that shall command George Frederick Cooke, and I put myself under his orders.'

"W——, one of the newcomers, who was mischievously filling up bumpers for Cooke, and persuading him, the moment after drinking that he neglected to drink, whispered me, 'I suppose then your orders will be sailing orders.' I begged him to desist from his sport, and he and his companions went off, professing that they were going to prepare for a ball.

"'A ball!' exclaimed Cooke, as they bade him good-night, and went off, 'they reel from the bottle to the ball! If ever I have an opportunity of quizzing these Yankees, I'll remember this. I'll not forget the drunken gentlemen in their dirty boots going to a ball! But it's just like everything else in the d—d country.'

"Mr. Wood, who was sufficiently under the influence of his own good wine not to see the uselessness of opposing Cooke, instead of laughing, began seriously to explain:

"'But, my dear sir, they are only going to change their dress before going to a ball.'

"'Don't talk to *me*, sir! Pretty fellows for the company of ladies, just from the tavern, the cigar, and the bottle!'

"'But, my dear sir——'

"Then Cooke would dash his fist on the table, with the tremendous 'Hear me, sir!' which always produced silence after a laugh at the ludicrous impropriety of his peremptory tone and manner.

"'They don't know what belongs to gentlemen, and have no idea of the decency and suavity of politeness.—My dear D—, sit down by me—don't leave me again. Didn't I throw out my voice this morning! Ah, ha!—haw! Ah, ha!—I astonished the Yankee actors!—I gave it them—I'll show these fellows what acting is!'

"*Wood.* 'You frightened some of our young men, sir; but they are clever lads, I'll assure you.'

"*C——.* 'Clever are they? I wonder how you are to find it out. But you're all alike!'

"*W——.* 'My dear sir, I have seen you act when you were surrounded by dire dogs.'

"*C——.* 'The worst of them, better than the best of you.'

"*W——.* 'Jack B——, now, he's a clever lad, but you won't say he's an actor. I love Jack, he's my friend, but he's a dire dog of an actor.'

"*C*——. 'He's your friend, is he? you take an odd way of showing your friendship. I feel inclined to be severe.' Turning to one near him: 'I'll cut up these Yankee actors, and their wooden god—don't leave me. O, the night I slept at Amboy—I never slept in my life before—poor Billy Lewis is dead—sixty-five—I thought I should have seen him again.'

"*W*——. 'Ah, sir, he was an actor!'

"*C*——. 'How do you know, sir?'

"*W*——. 'Why, my dear sir, I have seen him many a time.'

"*C*——. 'You see him! where should you see him?'

"*W*——. 'In England, sir—in London.'

"*C*——. 'And what then? What the more would *you* know from having seen him?' And then to another person, and in another tone, 'Didn't I throw out my voice this morning! I'll show them what acting is. They talk of their Cooper,' raising his voice furiously, 'their idol! their wooden god! Compare *me* to Cooper! Have not I stood the trial with John? What is your Cooper compared to Kemble!'

"*W*——. 'But, Mr. Cooke, you are supposing a comparison that no one has made—Mr. Cooper is a gentleman and a scholar——'

"*C——.* 'A scholar? How do you find that out? His scholarship is deep, it never appears.'

"*W——.* 'But as to comparison with you, no one thinks of making any——'

"*C——.* 'Sir, I have heard it. An actor!—he's no actor—a ranting mouther, that can't read a line! I appeal to you——'

"'Sir, Mr. Cooper is *my* friend——'

"He appeared to pay no attention to the reply, but ceased speaking of Cooper, and turned his abuse more particularly against Mr. Wood's acting, of which he knew nothing, as he had never seen him play, nor heard him recite a speech.

"While a servant by his desire went for a carriage, he continued this strain of abuse on any person whose image was presented to his mind, and particularly upon Americans, and their country, at the same time drinking what was officiously poured out for him, in that hurried and forced manner with which we have seen a nauseous drug thrown down the throat; when suddenly he looked at Mr. Wood, who sat opposite to him, and exclaimed:

"'Why don't you drink, sir? You don't drink.'

"'I am waiting,' pointing to a bottle of wine in a cooler, 'till *this* wine cools, sir.'

"'So—and give me the warm—d——d polite! but you are all alike—Cooper and Price and you are——'

"'Sir, I never allow a man, whatever his situation may be, to make use of such an appellation to me.'

"Cooke had made use of an expression which conveyed an idea of unfair dealing in respect to his engagement, and a term of vulgar insult; and now seeing a serious effect produced, immediately appeared to collect himself for a retreat. Mr. Wood proceeded:

"'If you think there is anything unfair on our part, in your Philadelphia engagement, Mr. Warren and myself will instantly annul it. Sir, you have made use of an appellation which I will not suffer any man to make use of to me.'

"Cooke disavowed all intention of disrespect, and backed out most manfully, until a perfect reconciliation took place. . . .

"During this visit to New York, Mr. Cooke exhibited himself at a tea-party. A number of ladies and gentlemen met, all anxious to see this extraordinary creature, and anticipating the pleasure to be derived, as they supposed, from his conversation, his humour, and his wit. Cooke, charged much higher with wine than with wit, and with that stiffness produced by the endeavour to counteract involuntary motion, was introduced into a large circle of gentlemen, distinguished for learning, or wit, or taste; and ladies, equally distinguished for those acquirements and endowments most valued in their sex.

"A part of the property of the tragedian which had been seized by the custom-house officers, under the non-importation law, had not been yet released, owing to some delay from necessary form, and this was a constant subject of irritation to him, particularly that they should withhold from him the celebrated cups presented to him by the Liverpool managers; and now his introductory speech among his expectant circle was addressed to one of the gentlemen, with whom he was acquainted, and was an exclamation without any prefatory matter, of 'They have stolen my cups!'

"The astonishment of such an assembly may be imagined. After making his bows with much circumspection, he seated himself, and very wisely stuck to his chair for the remainder of the evening; and he likewise stuck to his text, and his cups triumphed over every image that could be presented to his imagination.

"'Madam, they have stopped my cups. Why did they not stop my swords? No, they let my *swords* pass. But my cups will melt, and they have a greater love for silver than for steel. My swords would be useless with them; but they can melt my cups and turn them to dollars! And my Shakespeare—they had better keep that: they need his instruction, and may improve by him—if they know how to read him.'

"Seeing a print of Kemble in Rolla, he addressed it: 'Ah, John, are you there!' then turning to Master Payne, he, in his half-whispering manner, added, 'I don't want to die in this country—John Kemble will laugh.'

"Among the company was an old and tried revolutionary officer—a true patriot of '76.

"Hearing Cooke rail against the country and the government, he at first began to explain, and then to defend; but soon finding what his antagonist's situation was, he ceased opposition. Cooke continued his insolence, and finding that he was unnoticed, and even what he said in the shape of query unattended to, he went on:

"'That's right; you are prudent—the government may hear of it—walls have ears!'

"Tea was repeatedly presented to him, which he

refused. The little black girl with her *server* next offered him cake—this he rejected with some asperity. Fruit was offered to him, and he told the girl he was 'sick of seeing her face.' Soon after, she brought him wine. 'Why, you little black angel,' says Cooke, taking the wine, 'you look like the devil, but you bear a passport that would carry you unquestioned into Paradise.'

"The company separated early, and Master Payne happily resigned his visitor to the safe keeping of the waiters of the Tontine Coffee House.

"At Baltimore, as in every other city on the continent, the greatest admiration was shown of Mr. Cooke's talents as an actor, and the strongest desire to pay him every respect as a gentleman. But the same obstacles arose to the fulfilment of this wish as at every other place he had visited.

"In one instance, when a gentleman happened to mention that his family were among the first settlers of Maryland, he asked him if he had carefully preserved the family jewels. And on being questioned as to his meaning, replied, 'the chains and handcuffs.'

"The notoriety of his character preserved him from such returns as such language would have met if coming from other men; and this, perhaps, encouraged him to indulge what he called his propensity to sarcasm.

"At a dinner-party given in honour of him by Mr.——, he was led, still continuing his libations, to descant on Shakespeare, and the mode of representing his great characters; which he did eloquently, and to the delight of a large company. Suddenly, to the astonishment of them all, he jumped up, and exclaimed:

"'Who among you sent me that d——d anonymous letter?'

"'What do you mean, Mr. Cooke?'

"'You know what I mean. What have I done to offend you? Have I not treated ye all with more respect than ye deserved? And now to have a charge of so base a nature made against me!'

"'What do you complain of, Mr. Cooke?'

"'Sir, I am accused of falsehood. I am accused of making false assertions. I have received an anonymous letter containing this line alone, "Justify your words." Sir, my words are truth. What have I said that I cannot justify? I have perhaps been too keen upon the character of your country, but truth is the severest satire upon it. I am ready to justify what I have said!'

"Mr. ——, seeing his company thrown into confusion, and all harmony broken up, arose and expostulated with his guest, and finally hinted that the anonymous letter was a creation of his heated imagination. Cooke then resumed his seat, and fixing his eye on his host for some time, exclaimed, 'I have marked you, sir! I have had my eye upon you; it is time that your impertinence should be curbed!'

"This excessive licentiousness of speech, with the peculiar manner of the speaker, appeared so ludicrous, that the company burst into loud laughter, and Cooke, changing his manner, joined heartily with them, and again resumed his glass.

"Some time after, a gentleman told him that it was reported that Mr. Madison, the President of the United States, purposed to come from Washington to Baltimore, to see him act.

"'If he does, I'll be d—d if I play before him. What! I! George Frederick Cooke! who have acted before the majesty of Britain, play before your Yankee president! No!—I'll go forward to the audience, and I'll say, Ladies and gentlemen——'

"Here he was interrupted playfully by Mr. W——, who happened to be dressed in black.

"'Oh, no, Mr. Cooke, that would not be right in this country; you should say, Friends and fellow-citizens.'

"Cooke, surveying him contemptuously, cried, 'Hold your tongue, you d—d methodist preacher;' and then proceeded—'Ladies and gentlemen, the king of the Yankee-doodles has come to see me act; me, *me*, George Frederick Cooke! who have stood before my royal master George the Third, and received his imperial approbation! And shall I exert myself to play before one of his rebellious subjects, who arrogates kingly state in defiance of his master? No, it is degradation enough to play before rebels; but I'll not go on for the amusement of a king of rebels, the contemptible king of the Yankee-doodles!'

"This effusion only excited laughter, and he went on to expatiate on his deeds of arms in the war against the rebels; and every place in the neighbourhood where an action had been fought was the scene of his military achievements.

"His garrulity led him to talk of his domestic affairs, and to lament that he had no children; but shortly after, filling a bumper, he proposed the health of his eldest son, a captain in the 5th.

"'What is his name, Mr. Cooke?'

"'What is my name, sir?· George Frederick Cooke.'

"A short time after, his second son was proposed with a bumper.

"'What is his name, Mr. Cooke?'

"'What should it be, sir, but George Frederick Cooke?'

"With difficulty he was prevailed upon to get into a coach to return home to Baltimore. Still it was necessary that some one should attend him, and late at night his host performed that kind office. This offended Cooke, and he began to abuse him, and everything belonging to the country. This gentleman observing the stump of a tree near the wheel-track, as they passed through a grove, cautioned the coachman. 'What, sir, do you pretend to direct my servant?' cried Cooke. His companion humoured him by apologizing; but seeing the coachman driving too near the edge of a bridge, he again spoke to him.

"'This is too much,' cried Cooke; 'get out of my coach, sir!—out—stop, coachman!'

"'Drive on!'

"'Get out! Do you order my coachman? Get out, or this fist shall——'

"Mr. ——, who had been told Cooke's character, interrupted him by exclaiming:

"'Sit still, sir, or I'll blow your brains out this instant.'

"Cooke was petrified, and sat like a statue—but soon began with 'Has George Frederick Cooke come to this d——d country to be treated thus? Shall it be told in England!—Well, sir, if you will not get out, I will,' and he opened the door. Mr. —— was obliged to stop the coach, for fear of injury to Cooke, who tumbled himself out, and surlily sat down under a tree. With great difficulty his opposition was overcome, and Mr. ——, near daylight, got rid of his troublesome and turbulent guest by depositing him at his lodgings.

"Thus in every city the disposition to honour his talents was opposed by his unhappy habits, and it was found that, whatever he once might have been, he was no longer an agreeable associate for gentlemen, unless the bottle was kept out of sight."

But there was soon to be an end to this round of drunkenness, and mad fury, and grotesqueness. So wild and disorderly a life was not destined to endure long, and this American outburst hurried the whole to a conclusion. It would be impossible to give an idea of the extravagant alternations that marked his short stay in the country. No wonder that Byron should write of the strange record of his adventures, that "nothing like it has drenched the press. All green-room and tap-room. Drams and the drama — brandy, whisky punch, and latterly toddy, overflow every page."

After a series of attacks and recoveries that almost invariably followed when he returned to a sober course of life, he found it impossible to resist the seduction of fresh debauches, and at last, in September 1812, he expired at the age of fifty-seven, quite worn out.

CHAPTER VI.

Elliston.*

The looking at portraits of famous comedians seems to be entertainment almost second to that of seeing them on the stage. No such intellectual pleasure is of course to be gathered from photographs,—which bear both portrait and spectator downwards, and show how far below the high standard we had dreamed of must be the originals. This disagreeable effect is owing to the suppression of all that is intelligent, and to the development of what is earthly and material—owing to the enforced attitude and impassive mood required by the process. To those who so often repeat that a photograph must be the best kind of likeness, it can therefore be said that the mere outline of face and figure is but an element of resemblance; and that expression under the most favourable emotion—as when the orator is kindling with his subject, or when the most agreeable faculties are

* Born 1774, died 1831.

awakened—is a far more essential point. Hence it is that between photography and art there is a sort of sunken fence which by no ingenuity or amount of improvement can ever be crossed.

Among theatrical portraits, on the contrary, are found the most favourable specimens of the painter's craft. There is a vivacity, a life, a variety not found in other likenesses. There has been a regular line of actors' portrait painters—Hogarth Zoffany, Harlow, and De Wilde, perhaps the most versatile and practised of all. It is impossible to give an idea of the range of expression, the infinite intelligence of the faces thus happily preserved. The full-length of Edwin as the "Marquis" in 'A Midnight Hour,' at South Kensington, is a happy example, and exhibits an airy ease, an aristocratic refinement, as well as a hint of that slight exaggeration of bearing which Lamb insisted was necessary to true comedy, as opposed to the more exact imitation or "realism" which is the highest aim of our day. In presence of such pictures we enjoy comedy at second hand, and indeed have a glimpse of comedy itself.

These reflections are more particularly suggested by the portrait of an admirable comedian, Robert Elliston, which hangs upon the walls of the Garrick

Club, and which, like so many of its fellows, is delightful to look on—being the complement, as it were, of his life, which has a dash of one of Congreve's gay heroes. To such a career it would be unadvisable to apply the rule and square of order or morality; that can be done by the proper appraisers—the students and regulators of Society, to whom such are sadly amenable. But there is a comedy side to life for which a later generation makes an audience, and which is to be treated as Elia so indulgently justified the loose but sparkling pieces of Congreve and Wycherley, as belonging to an artificial realm of their own, where no moral law obtained. Something of the same immunity is enjoyed by these *viveurs* in the flesh, whose derelictions are carried off pleasantly, and scarcely felt as wrongs by even the victim. Nowadays this species of airy comedy has passed away from the stage, because it has passed away from real life. Society has grown strict, and insists that all should be subject to the same discipline and rules. No agreeable Sheridan puts off the creditor with a good story, or tricks him after a fashion the creditor himself must smile at.

Elliston was one of the comedians of real as well as of stage life; he was always playing 'Mirabel' or 'Archer,' in the street or the house; and it would be hard to say whether he brought these manners with him from the drawing-room to the stage, or from the stage to the drawing-room. These two categories were indeed not separated by any hard line, but were blended. His handsome figure, brightly intelligent face, in which lurked a roguish insinuation, or tone of voice conveyed a sort of second intention, as it were, that sort of legitimate *double entendre* which in its true sense makes half the charm of comedy. He was always gay and gallant, making comedy speeches off the stage, and dealing out magnified flourishes to all the world. Drunken habits, and other indecencies, to say nothing of vanity and the pride of managerial prerogative, turned what was merely histrionic exaggeration into positive eccentricity, and towards the end of his life the confusion between the two states of being was complete.

Such a hero, when an insinuating youth, of course ran away from home to go on the stage. Though his father was a watchmaker, his other connections were respectable, and his uncle a dignitary of one of the Oxford Colleges. His graceful figure, manners, and intelligent style soon advanced him in the profession, or rather in *both* professions, for society was henceforth found to be as profitable and agreeable a one as his official calling. His marriage had a sort of comedy flavour; a rather *passée* dancing mistress at Bath, Miss Fleming, having fallen in love with him. It was her assistant, however, that was the object of his attentions, whom he eventually married. His wife proved an excellent, amiable woman, almost too tolerant of the levities and failings of the gay husband, who indulged in the fashionable excesses of high play, deep drinking, and gallantry. The average course of his domestic life, or the sober records of his professional engagements, would have little interest for the reader, and belong to the regular annals of the stage. It is a study of *character*, eccentric, buoyant, and exceptional, that is presented here. After his reputation was made he began to attract attention by a sort of extravagance, and to court the attention and sympathy of the public by devices outside the line of his profession. This was owing to his vanity, which had become egregious, and which led him into the delusion that he was of such importance that his proceedings off the stage were equally interesting with his legitimate performances on the boards. The agreeable comedian was unhappily gifted with a turn for speech-making, which led him, like so many of his brethren, to turn the stage into a rostrum, or tribune, from which he could communicate his grievances and opinions to the audience. The latter, from curiosity and the desire of novelty, is naturally ready to encourage such exhibitions, which have often a dramatic character of their own, though a character not in harmony with the place.

In July 1805, a piece by Andrew Cherry—a facetious actor who once ended his letter "You cannot make two bites of A Cherry"—was brought out at the Haymarket, and was a complete failure. Elliston, however, who had taken a perverse interest in it, determined that it should have a second trial on the following night, when it met with even a more hostile reception. During its progress, when loud disapprobation was being expressed, it was noticed that the excited patron of the piece had singled out a gentleman in the boxes, who was conspicuous in expressing his opinion, and half unsheathing his stage sword, hurled defiance at him. At the close of the performance, when the curtain had fallen in a storm of disapproval, a long delay succeeded, which was followed by the abrupt appearance of Mr. Elliston, who was much excited, and appeared to arrive fresh from some scene of scuffle or confusion. He thus addressed the audience:—

"LADIES AND GENTLEMEN,

"I am at present considerably agitated, not so much by what has occurred before the curtain, as by a circumstance which has just taken place behind it. [Here there was *universal consternation and anxiety.*]

"I have, ever since I had the honour of appearing before the public, enjoyed such a share of its favour and patronage, that no consideration whatever shall deter me from speaking the truth. The number of those who supported the present piece last night induced me to give it out for a second representation, although, I *solemnly declare* (*pressing his hand on his heart*), contrary to my own opinion (*mixture of plaudits and disapprobation*). It *must now clearly appear to every unprejudiced person* that the sense of the house is decidedly against it (*bursts of applause and some faint hisses*). I therefore, with your permission, beg to substitute 'The Dramatist' for it to-morrow night" (*very loud plaudits, with some few hisses*).

The passage "it must now clearly appear to every *unprejudiced* person, that the sense of the house, &c.," is deliciously Ellistonian, and touches the true " note" of his character.

Much speculation was excited by the exordium: and it was soon known that something extraordinary had taken place behind the scenes. Elliston, it seems, had attacked the performers, and, in "a scolding and denouncing manner," had attributed the failure to their bad acting. This intemperateness was naturally resented; and Mathews angrily replied that every one "had played as well as Elliston, if not better." The latter promptly gave his brother the lie, and, according to the report, was instantly knocked down: as he rose and tried to retaliate, he received a second blow, which again prostrated him. This unseemly contest might have gone on for some time, had not some peacemaker reminded the combatants that the audience were waiting. Threatening all round him with vengeance, the excited Elliston, wearing all the marks of the fray on his person, then rushed before the audience and made his enigmatical statement.

The matter could not, of course, be allowed to rest there, and on the following day, the assaulted actor, as eager to present himself before readers as he was before hearers, wrote a letter to the papers.

The underlined passages are pleasantly significant of the "euphuistic" side of his character, and the notion that "those who knew him best must be sensible that he was *not likely to be seen in any such state of degradation,*" i.e., prostrated by a knock-down blow, would have delighted Lamb himself.

"Sir,

"Some extraordinary misrepresentation having appeared with respect to an occurrence at this theatre last night, in which I happened to be a party, I owe it in justice to myself to require that the facts may be correctly stated.

"It is true that a momentary altercation did arise between Mr. Mathews and myself immediately after the dropping of the curtain last night, which was attended by some warmth on both sides; but it is not true, as has been asserted, that I was 'knocked down twice,' nor indeed that I was 'knocked down' at all. *Nor is it true that I was placed in any situation humiliating to my feelings as a man, nor in the slightest degree derogatory to my character as a gentleman. Without using any idle professions as to my own means of self-defence, I may be pardoned when I say that those who know me best must be sensible that I am not likely to be seen in any such state of degradation.*

"Neither is it true that this disagreement grew out of any assertion made by me, that Mr. Mathews, or that any gentleman of this theatre, had done less than his duty in supporting the piece which had not met with the public approbation. What the circumstances were it would be useless and perhaps impertinent in me to obtrude on the public attention. It is enough to say that Mr. Mathews and myself have every likelihood of being good friends, and that, were we not so, it would be difficult to find any man more ready than myself to subscribe to the professional excellence of Mr. Mathews, and to acknowledge the fidelity and zeal with which he at all times exerts his talents for the benefit of the theatre, and for the amusement of the public." . . .

He added a sort of testimonial to this letter, signed by the two Palmers and some other "bystanders during the accidental difference," as they styled themselves, which was to the effect that it was "totally void of foundation" that Mr. Elliston had been knocked down, and concluding with a sort of Pickwickian declaration that "no circumstance took place which was in any respect dishonourable to that gentleman or indeed to either party." Mathews, to Elliston's infinite annoyance, took the more dignified course of remaining silent, declining either to accept or contradict Elliston's version of the matter. The rather fine distinction was probably made that Mr. Elliston had indeed come to the ground, though not from a blow of Mathews. The matter could hardly remain there, and a Mr. Philips waited on Mathews' "friend," Sir John Carr, to demand an apology for the assault. This was refused, on the ground that the blow had been returned; and, as both parties were firm, the only solution of the difficulty seemed to be the one then fashionable among gentlemen. Suddenly, to the amazement of those who were looking on, a highly irrelevant issue was tendered and accepted, and Mr. Mathews was asked to declare in writing that " he had never endeavoured to injure Mr. Elliston in the opinion of the managers of the Haymarket Theatre or *any one of them*," or that he had "never countenanced any party in hostility to Mr. Elliston's interests." In return for which declaration, in whose legal particularity Elliston seemed to look for the satisfaction he could not otherwise obtain, the latter on the same day declared that he had been mistaken "in *the suspicions he had formed* as to any injurious conduct," on the part of Mr. Mathews, and regretted he should have so far wronged Mr. Mathews as to have entertained any of the kind. There is nothing more amusing in the whole annals of gentlemen's difficulties; though the "Pickwickian sense" of originally hostile declarations has become almost a proverb, it has never taken so entertaining a shape. The two actors, who had been schoolfellows, were reconciled, and when they appeared on the stage in some piece where they had to shake hands, the late unseemly quarrel was recognized by the audience, and a hearty burst of applause greeted this symbolical token of friendship. Thus the affair ended.

A sort of omnivorous passion for directing theatres had taken possession of this singular being, and he had soon collected into his single hands the reins of management of nearly half a dozen different houses. Indeed so overpowering was this fancy, that any sort of showman's exhibition that came into the market became, as it were, fish for his net, and he could not refrain from offering for dwarfs, circuses, monsters, &c. This curious taste could be accounted for, as these various offices of command presented so many opportunities of exercising the show of authority, speeches, and circumlocutions in which he delighted. He thus secured theatres at Liverpool, Birmingham—the "Royal Circus," which he converted into the more imposing Surrey Theatre, the Olympic, and later the great house of Drury Lane itself. Here, as may be imagined, he revelled in dignity, and speeched to his heart's content.

It was not, indeed, in his orthodox relations to the drama, but in his dealings with his audience, that his quaint gifts were exhibited. The presence of the crowd, the lights, the glitter, above all some commotion or excitement, seemed to call forth those curious arts which the rudely organized might class as "humbug," but which were in truth specimens of a high kind of art.—That they were removed from the disagreeable category just named, is proved by the success which almost invariably attended their exertion. We can hear him for instance in an emergency when a popular actor, set down for a particular part, had not appeared on the stage. This truant player's name was Carles,—it is Mrs. Mathews who tells the story :—

"The audience began to show its disapprobation in a noisy way; and 'Carles! Carles!' was the popular demand—a demand which Mr. Elliston was not backward to answer in his own way, and coming promptly forward with his most profound bow, respectfully, though haughtily, inquired of the '*Ladies* and Gentlemen' what was 'their *pleasure.*'

"Several voices vociferated, '*Carles!*' Elliston knitted his brows with excessive earnestness, affecting to be confounded by the noise, and, with increasing gravity, again desired to be acquainted with the occasion of the extraordinary tumult, adding, with something like command in his tone, '*One at a time*, if you please.' Again the popular cry was audible to those who 'had ears to hear.' One malcontent, raising his voice, however, louder than the rest, enforced Mr. Elliston's attention, and, fixing his eyes suddenly upon the man, the manager then turned his face from him for a moment, and haughtily *begging pardon of the rest of the pit*, added, 'Let me hear what *this gentleman* has to say;' and pointing to the turbulent individual in question, observed sternly, '*Now*, sir, I'll attend to *you—first*, if the rest of the *gentlemen* will allow me;' and here he made a stiff bow to the *gentleman* in question. All now became suddenly silent, and the selected person sat down, looking rather sheepish at the distinction shown him above his fellows, and Mr. Elliston, stooping over the orchestra, and fixing his eyes, like a browbeating barrister, on his victim, thus emphatically addressed his chosen man:

"'*Now*, sir, be so good as to inform me *what* it is *you require?*'

"The man, still abashed at being thus singled out for particular notice, in rather a subdued tone, but affecting his former valour, answered— 'Carles! Carles!'

"'Oh! *Carles!!!*' exclaimed Elliston, in a tone of surprise, as if only at that moment aware of the cause of dissatisfaction. 'Oh! ah! you want *Mr. Carles?* Is *that* what you say, sir?'

"'*Yes*,' responded the Pit-ite, with renewed confidence; 'his name's in the bill!'

"'Very *good*, sir!' said the manager, who throughout carried himself with the air of one who felt himself the injured party, 'I understand you now. You are right, so far, sir,—Mr. Carles's name is in the bill.'

"Here Mr. Elliston was interrupted by others who repeated—

"'Yes! yes!—his name's in the bill!—his name's in the bill!'

"'*Gentlemen!* with *your* leave, I will say a few words.' (All was again silent, and the manager's earnestness and dignity increased as he proceeded.) 'I admit that Mr. Carles's name *is* in the bill—I don't wish to deny it, but' (and here he assumed a solemnity of face and voice, and with his deepest tragedy-manner impressively observed)—'*But*, are you to be reminded of the many accidents that may intervene between the morning's issuing of *that bill*, and the evening's fulfilment of its promise? Is it requisite to remind the enlightened and thinking portion of the public here assembled (and he took a sweeping glance round the house), that the chances and changes of human life are dependent on *circumstances* and not upon *ourselves?*'

" Here the 'enlightened' exclaimed, 'Aye, aye! bravo!' and Mr. Elliston, gaining courage from this slight manifestation of sympathy, turned himself once more to his man with renewed *hauteur*, crying sharply, 'And *you*, sir, you who are so *loud* in your demand for Mr. Carles, cannot *you* also imagine that his absence may be occasioned by some dire distress, some occurrence not within human foresight to anticipate or divert? Can you not picture to yourself the possibility of Mr. Carles at this moment lying upon a sick—nay, perhaps a *dying* bed—surrounded by his weeping children and his agonized wife!' (Mr. Carles was a bachelor)—'whose very bread depends upon the existence of an affectionate, devoted husband and father—and who *may* be deprived of his exertions and support for ever? Is it so *very* difficult to imagine a scene like this taking place at the very moment you are calling for him so imperiously to appear before you—selfishly desirous of your present amusement, and unmindful of his probable danger!' (great and general applause). 'And *you*, sir, will perhaps *repeat* your demand to have Mr. Carles brought before you! Are you a husband? are you a father?'

"'Shame! shame!' resounded now from every part of the pit.

"'You are *right*, sir,' resumed the manager; 'you are *quite* right. It *is* a shame; I blush at such inhumanity!'

"'Turn him out! turn him out!' was now generally vociferated, even by those who had originally joined in the objectionable demand; and Elliston, choosing to receive this suggestion as a *question* addressed to himself, promptly replied with the most dignified assent—

"'*If* you *please!*'

"In the next moment the offending individual

was lifted above the heads of his brother malcontents, and, in spite of his vehement remonstrances and struggles, hoisted across the pit, actually ejected, and the door closed upon him by his removers. Mr. Elliston, who had waited the result with great composure, now bowed *very low*, while he received the general applause of the house and retired in grave triumph."

More characteristic still is his device on his benefit night at Worcester. For this solemnity he had issued a stupendous programme, announcing as the chief feature a magnificent display of fireworks *on the stage!* This novelty caused great excitement and much ingenious anticipation, owing to the conceived impossibility of introducing pyrotechnical effects—at least of such pretension as he had advertised—within the walls of a theatre. The airy comedian, however, gave the matter no thought until a day or two before the event— when all tickets had been taken. He then artfully began to hint to the landlord of the property— a worthy man, much respected in the place—some grave forebodings as to the dangers of such an exhibition, and so skilfully that the owner became alarmed and positively forbade the presentation of a performance so perilous to his interests. Elliston protested, and with much vehement indignation spoke of "his being committed to the public," of his honour engaged, and the like. The landlord was inflexible, and could only be prevailed on to keep the matter secret until the night. A crowded house assembled when the evening came round—drawn a good deal by the actor's own popularity, but more excited by the promise of the unusual entertainment held out. In a conspicuous box was seen the worthy landlord of the theatre, naturally a shy and retiring man, induced to attend by the beneficiaire's persuasions. The performance began and proceeded. Elliston exerted all his abilities, and the programme was being gradually got through, when the audience began to grow impatient for the promised entertainment. Cries of "The Fireworks! The Fireworks!" were raised, of which no notice was at first taken—as though it was some vulgar interruption from overcrowding, or other cause. The cries, however, growing more persistent, and finally swelling into an uproar, could not be further ignored. Then Elliston, putting on his great manner, came forward. Then came the usual pantomime—surprise, admirably depicted, lifting the eyebrows—a wish to hear every one. The fireworks?—

He at last apprehended the cause of this discontent, and proceeded to his explanation. He had made the most elaborate arrangements for a magnificent pyrotechnic display — had left nothing undone: but at the last moment came the reflection—what of the *danger*! The number of young, tender girls—of respectable matrons—all collected to do *him* honour—what if the theatre should take fire and be burnt to the ground—the property too of one of the best and worthiest of men, whom they *all* knew—and whom he knew. Here he pointed out the landlord, who was overwhelmed with confusion. He then publickly appealed to him, to say if he had not interposed for the protection of his property; and having thus artfully diverted attention from himself, proceeded to launch out into an eloquent panegyric on his merits. The audience were gradually soothed into good-humour—the ladies —being convinced that they had escaped a great danger—taking his side. "BUT," he said in conclusion, "But—ladies and gentlemen, I am happy to say I have made arrangements that will in some way make up for this disappointment—BAND!" looking down into the orchestra, where three wretched fiddlers furnished the whole strength of

the music—" Band! Play up 'God Save the
King' directly!" Under the spell of this curious
fascination—that genuine belief in himself—every
one in the house rose. He stood there in an attitude
of loyalty almost devotional, while that stirring air
was played; and then, as though he had done more
than he had covenanted—retired.

On another occasion at Birmingham, when his
theatrical affairs were in a very disastrous condition, he again conjured successfully with the same
charm. He had announced a "Bohemian, of unexampled Strength and Stature," who, amongst
other evolutionary feats, would display his facile
manipulation of a huge stone, of near a ton weight,
which he was to handle like a tennis-ball! The
"Bohemian" was stated as having been received
with favour and distinction in various Rhenish
States, and had actually felled an ox by a blow of
his naked fist, to lighten the *ennui* of a German
princess.

"The *Bohemian*, 'begot of nothing but vain
phantasy,' being, in other words, the offspring of
the manager's imagination, might indeed fairly
have been denominated a prodigy. Typical of
himself, the 'Bohemian' was advertised in gigantic letters, while sundry portraits, which had been

originally executed for the proprietors of the 'Saracen's Head' Inn, London, were placarded about the town, with the sub-lineation, 'THE BOHEMIAN!'

"The Birmingham people, who were beginning to sicken at tragedy, were wonderfully revived by this extimulation; the Bohemian, with his fist, was certainly 'a hit,' and the edifice was as full on the night of his promised appearance as though the Emperor of Austria himself had been expected. The play, 'Pizarro,' had but a poor chance—'The Bohemian! The Bohemian!' from the tongues of the spectators, completely drowned the words of the actors,—which, with considerable foresight, they had only half studied for the occasion. Down fell the curtain, and 'The Bohemian!' instantaneously broke out with fresh violence. The fiddlers struck up 'The Battle of Prague,' and every nerve was now attuned to the pancratic efforts which had been promised.

"At this juncture, Elliston, pale with consternation, which would have extorted pity from the original Saracen himself, stepped forward, and, with suppliant palms, addressed the assembly:

"'The Bohemian has deceived me!' said he—'*that* I could have pardoned; but he has deceived my friends—he has deceived *you!*'—at which he buried his face in his handkerchief; but to hide what emotion we will not hazard a guess. 'The Bohemian, I repeat, has deceived us—*he is not here;*' a certain smouldering now agitated the body of spectators. Elliston went on—'And the man, *of whatever name or nation he may be*, who violates his word, commits an offence which——' here an outbreak took place which completely annihilated the rest of his aphoristic sentence. He then proceeded :

"'Anxious for your gratification, I entered into correspondence with the faithless foreigner, who was this day to have appeared.' (A yell, which, in another place, would be denominated *ironical cheers*.) 'The correspondence, ladies and gentlemen, is in my pocket.' (An incredulous laugh.) 'I'll read it to you.' Here he produced a variety of papers resembling letters. ('Read! read!—No! no!—Imposition!') 'Here they are,' continued Elliston, with one of his most cunning looks; 'does any gentleman present read German?—if so, would he honour me by stepping forward?' (A scream of merriment.) 'Am I left alone? Then I'll translate it for you.' ('No! no! enough! Go on, Elliston!') 'I obey; the correspondence shall *not* be read'—here he deliberately replaced the bundle in his pocket—'but, ladies and gentlemen,' continued he, with a smile which could have levelled the Andes, 'the *stone* is here! You shall see it!' (A volcanic burst.) 'You shall yet be satisfied; you are my patrons, and have a right to demand it. Shall the stone be produced?' (Cries of 'The stone! the stone!') Here the manager winked his grey eye at the fiddlers, who again hastily betook themselves to 'The Battle of Prague,' when up sprang the curtain, disclosing a sand-rock, which, for weight and magnitude, would positively have made 'Bohemia nothing!' and bearing a scroll, '*This is the Stone!*' Good-humour, even confidence, seemed restored. Here was indeed *the stone*, and imagination did all the rest."

The variety of his extravagance was always infinite. On one occasion he announced to his surprised patrons, that he had been given to understand that his Royal Highness the Prince Regent would confer on him the honour of knighthood, and that when he next appeared before them the bill would probably run "Sir John Falstaff by *Sir Robert Elliston.*" There was no doubt he was sincere in these extraordinary flourishes, and that when he found himself for the moment the centre of attraction, the lights, the faces diverted to him, he felt himself transported into a sort of fairy realm, where all things possible became real, and his loftiest and most soaring dreams assumed consistence. The little brief authority in which he was dressed seemed to stretch beyond the walls of the theatre. A most characteristic specimen of his "greater style" was a valedictory address to the Leicester audience. There is a freshness and originality in his turns, and certainly a grandeur which he tempered by condescension. It will be seen how admirably he carried off the want of coherence in such addresses by importing a sort of fervour.

"Ladies and gentlemen," he said, " the painful moment of our separation has arrived. That I have been indulgent to you, there is no denying —some say I have *spoilt* you. It was in this city, ladies and gentlemen, that that remarkable character, Cardinal Wolsey, laid down his glory and his bones. Can I do better than employ his words in honour of our present illustrious Regent? 'He is a prince of a most royal carriage, and hath a princely heart;' to this let me add, God bless him!

" I would remind you that your late worshipful mayor, Mr. Wilcox, and myself, were schoolfellows. The loss of him, you yourselves cannot deplore more than I do, and now 'beyond that bourne from which no traveller returns,' we have only to hope that he is happy!" (Here the orator wiped his eyes.) "Ladies and gentlemen, once again I bid you respectfully—affectionately, farewell!"

So when two rival heroines—" the Giroux" and "the Taylor"—engaged together at his Surrey-side theatre, in pantomime, had each their band of admirers, who crowded the house for nightly riots and confusion, the crafty Elliston stimulated the jealousy and partisanship which was so favourable to his treasury. Every night the storm raged; the hackney coaches of the hostile fair ones were attended to the stage door by mobs, and saluted with cheers and hisses, while within the theatre fierce battles were fought. Elliston, enchanted at the opportunities thus offered, was in his element, speeching from the stage, and inflaming while he affected to control. An appeal which "the Giroux" made to her admirers was known to have been the manager's composition. It is Ellistonian all over.

"Surrey Theatre.

"Miss Giroux, deeply deploring the display of a spirit in this theatre which, however flattering, is by no means calculated to serve her who is the object of it, presumes publicly to declare that she has, neither personally nor otherwise, encouraged any hostility to the professional pretensions of a young person called Taylor.

"Miss Giroux takes the liberty to request that the enlightened portion of the British public, which does her the honour to approve her performances, will add to so proud a distinction the favour of abstaining from an unseemly contest, nor

'Mix with hired slaves, bravos, and common stabbers;'

but allow, at once, MIND to triumph over MATTER!

"N.B.—Miss Giroux is not aware, that in this generous nation it is disreputable to be either a Jew or a foreigner; but attempts have been made to fix on her the *stigma* of both! Miss Giroux is by no means a Jew, and has the happiness, moreover, of being born an English young lady."

When he thought matters had gone far enough, and the excitement was beginning to flag, he came forward and announced that "*on the following night he would himself give judgment in the case!*" And when he appeared on this important occasion, he called haughtily to the prompter, "Bring me a chair!" and a sort of judicial throne was placed for him, into which he sank, and began gravely to "sum up." Burlesque could not farther go—but on the rude natives of the "Surrey side" such fine irony was thrown away. Their coarse natures could only appreciate vulgar matter of fact. The "giving judgment in the case" was scarcely found intelligible, and produced fresh uproar. For many more nights manager and mob contended with each other in extravagance and riot, until the confusion became a nuisance to the neighbourhood, and the authorities were compelled to interfere.

The story oftenest told to illustrate the magnificence of his self-delusion, was the one associated with the dramatic pageant which he got up at Drury Lane in honour of the King's coronation. It was sumptuously produced, and extraordinarily successful. The excitement, the applause, the hand, some coronation robes which he wore—Elliston representing his Majesty—and the elaborate theatrical state, all in his honour—coextensive in some degree with his actual authority as the employer or master of all these stage mercenaries—combined to settle the delusion in his wits that he was the King! As the roars of applause burst from the packed galleries and pit, and the stately monarch came down to the front, last in the procession, he felt himself transported with pride and gratitude, and said aloud, "*Bless ye my people!*" He later struck a medal for distribution among the audience, in imitation of the greater precedent at Westminster.

It was curious to note how lofty a dignity, with something approaching to meanness, were found in this singular character. Yet there seemed to be nothing inconsistent in this combination, both extremes being in harmony with the nature of Robert William Elliston. He ranged from the full-blown dignity of lessee of one of the great theatres, to the directorship of what was little more than a barn at Buxton, with the same complacency. "It was my fortune," says Lamb, "to encounter him near St. Dunstan's Church on the morning of his election to that high office. Grasping my hand with a look of significance, he only uttered, 'Have you heard the news?'—then with another look following up the blow, he subjoined

'I am the future manager of Drury Lane Theatre.' Breathless as he saw me, he stayed not for congratulation or reply, but mutely stalked away, leaving me to chew upon his new-blown dignities at leisure. In fact, nothing could be said to it. . . . This was in his *great* style." The truth was he was so settled in the conviction of his own elegant superiority, that the mere material accidents of size or state were indifferent to *him*. He lived in the delightful dream that they must also be matters of indifference to those who were content to accept him. Thus in his little booth at Leamington he would treat his " patrons," with a pleasant absence of ceremony, according to his humour, and would invite them to such pieces as 'Three Weeks after Marriage,' " with only himself, one lady, a couple of amateur tradesmen, and the doorkeeper's son" to fill the various parts. It was enough that *he* was the entertainment. In another piece, where there was a more serious deficiency, he condescended to greater exertion, and delivered the words of nearly every character. The amateur tradesmen, doorkeeper's son, &c., were enjoined to watch him, to go off, or come on at his signals, while he repeated their portion of the dialogue, as though they were marionettes which he worked. The device was perfectly successful.

A certain decay, however, always attends the career of "pleasant creatures" such as Elliston. There is a toleration of these exuberances—as in the case of Sheridan and Hook—so long as the sense of novelty lasts, but they must then accept degradation, which is all the grosser, because contrasted with their airy natures, fondly supposed to be privileged. On account of some slight arrear in his rent, he was summarily thrust out of his great theatre at Drury. This at least was the pretext, though it is probable that the amateur directors, the Douglas Kinnairds and the rest, were eager to close their connection with one who indulged in such curious antics. The deposed monarch submitted with dignity to his altered state, and retired to his old house on the Surrey-side. It was there that he told Douglas Jerrold, who was pressing for some remuneration on the astounding success of 'Black-eyed Susan'—which had run over two hundred nights—that " he ought *to get his friends* to present him with a piece of plate." This has often been told in this detached shape, as a specimen of the ingratitude and rapaciousness of managers. But how different does it appear when read in connection with the character we have just been considering. It is really appropriate, and in an Elliston not unfeeling. It was tho airy speech of a gay gentleman in comedy —some Chesterfield on the stage.

Nothing daunted by his reverse he gave his little senate laws from the boards of the Surrey. Here he again speeched and descanted.

"On one evening," says Mr. Raymond,* "pending the representation of a very serious piece, a sailor elevated, in every sense of the word, frequently interrupted the progress of the play, and annoyed the audience by exclamations of dissatisfaction and sundry noises peculiar to gentlemen of the sea. At length Elliston appeared on the stage :—

"'May I know the cause of this unseemly clamour?' asked he.

"(*Voice from the gallery*).—' It's this here sailor what makes the row.'

"'A British sailor!—the glory of our country's annals!—the safeguard of our homes and families! What is it he asks?'

"'Rule Britannia!' roared the tar.

"'You shall have it!' emphatically pronounced the manager. 'Of what ship, comrade?'

* In his pleasant memoir from which is taken much of this article.

"'The *Haggermemnon*,' again roared our son of Neptune.

"'Ladies and gentlemen,' continued the manager, advancing a few steps forward with impertubable assurance, 'on Monday next, a nautical, national, allegorical sketch will be represented at this theatre, entitled, "The British Flag!" in which the whole strength of the company will be employed. The music expressly composed by Mr. Blewitt. Give 'em "Rule Britannia,"' concluded he, with a nod to the musicians. 'Bring your companions here on Monday,' cried Elliston, with a wink at the sailor, which having done he strode off the stage."

'Rule Britannia' was immediately sung "by the whole strength of the company," and the play was resumed. As to the nautical sketch, it is needless to say this was *the momentary suggestion of the manager's untiring fancy.*

"On another evening too many persons having been admitted to the gallery, occasioned much altercation, and totally prevented the performers from being heard.

"Elliston came forward as usual, and thus addressed the audience :—

"'Ladies and gentlemen,—I take the liberty of

addressing you. It is of rare occurrence that I deem it necessary to place myself in juxtaposition with you. (*Noise in the gallery.*) When I said juxtaposition, I meant *vis-à-vis*. (*Increased noise in the gallery.*) When I uttered the words *vis-à-vis*, I meant *contactability*. Now let me tell you that *vis-à-vis* (it is a French term) and contactability (which is a truly English term) very nearly assimilate to each other. (*The disturbance above redoubled.*) Gentlemen!—Gentlemen! I am really ashamed of your conduct. It is unlike a Surrey audience. Are you aware that I have in this establishment most efficient peace-officers at my immediate disposal? Peace-officers, gentlemen, mean persons necessary in time of war.

"'One word more,' said he, returning; 'if that tall gentleman, in the carpenter's cap, will sit down [pointing to the pit], the little girl behind him, in red ribbons (you, my love, I mean), will be able to see the entertainment.'

"This oration produced the desired effect, and Elliston after bowing most respectfully, as he always did when he had made an impudent speech, retired to spend his *afternoon.*"

Even drunkenness used to affect him in a highly fantastic way, and was different from the intoxication of ordinary men. It was more like the freaks of extravagance. No such singular scene, as the following could be conceived.

"The 2nd of May was fixed for a royal visit to the theatre. The King had held a drawing-room at Buckingham Palace on the morning of this day, and a few untoward events, added to the fatigue consequent on the ceremony, found his Majesty not in the most serene temper of mind on his return to Carlton House. By the King's desire, however, the captain of the escort, Lord William Lennox, rode immediately abreast the window of the royal carriage; an arrangement wisely made, for, on the morning, as the august party were passing the entrance to the stable-yard, a missile was projected at the King's person, which struck the captain of the escort. The gallant captain, however, shook his plumes, and all was well again.

"The rush into the theatre was tremendous. Considerable uproar, from various parts of the house, ensued, on disputed seats and packed benches, which, just as the King entered his box, being at spring-tide, his Majesty felt impressed was chiefly directed towards his own person. The Lord Chamberlain at once perceived the King's feeling, and instantly requested his vice-official, the Marquess Graham, to descend, and at once see the manager, that the uproar might be appeased by explanation. Lord Graham now hastened to the stage, where, meeting Elliston in full costume, and totally forgetting he was accosting a *crowned head,* exclaimed—

"'Mr. Elliston, this is disgraceful! You should have prevented this excess. The King is vexed, and will never again come to Drury Lane.'

"This speech, addressed as it was with considerable acrimony to Elliston, surrounded by many distinguished strangers and followers of the court, besides troops of his *own subjects,* very sensibly nettled him. He replied with equal warmth, but ten times greater dignity; when, at that moment, espying Lord William Lennox, he added—

"'Now, my Lord Graham, I have a friend; my wounded honour I shall place in the hands of Lord William;' which having said, he sweepingly led the way across the stage into his own private room; the captain of the guard following. Lord William, *en cuirass;* Elliston 'with his sword by his side;' full bottles and empty bottles—the long-necked Champagne and the rush-covered Curaçoa —plays, poetry, and the 'London Gazette'— fans, tippets, and handkerchiefs 'of the smallest spider's web,' formed the strangest confusion of effects.

"Elliston now entered grandiloquently into the nature of his grievance; but his friend soon perceiving that, though the vice-chamberlain might have wounded the dignity of the manager, Moët had clearly disordered his wits; he gave him, therefore, certain advice, which produced the following:

"'You are right, my lord. The *deputy* has affronted me, and a *deputy* shall reply to it. My stage-manager shall take up the question in its present shape. I shall meet no one but the Lord Chamberlain himself. My lord, a glass of Madeira?'

"The curtain had fallen on the night's entertainment—the King had returned to Carlton House—the escort to the Horse Guards; and it being now one o'clock of the following morning, the captain had doffed his leathern pantaloons and huge jackboots, preparing himself for repose, when a sharp knock was heard at his chamber door.

"'Who's there?' interrogated the captain, not a little disinclined to intrusion at such an hour.

"'One of his Majesty's secretaries of state, my lord, on urgent business,' replied the sergeant.

"'What can it mean?' murmured the Horse Guardsman.

"'I know not, my lord, but he said it was on business—"vital," I think was the word. The gentleman is now in the sitting-room.'

"To the sitting-room Lord William immediately proceeded, when he beheld, seated in an arm-chair, no less a personage than the monarch of Drury Lane—King William Elliston! in the same court gear in which he had a few hours before attended the monarchy of Great Britain; but a little damaged.

"'I have taken the liberty,' observed Elliston, in a manner even more impressive than his usual delivery, 'during your lordship's delay, of ordering a weak glass of brandy and water from the canteen.'

"Here the manager paused to sip his mixture. 'My lord, we must go out this very morning—I am steady to my purpose,' added he, reeling actually in his chair.

"Lord William now perceived that a confused recollection of Lord Graham's affront had brought Elliston, drunk as a lord, from the theatre to the Horse Guards: there to renew the story, and pass the remainder of a quiet evening.

"Lord William now pursued the same policy he had taken in the manager's room; namely, representing that it was utterly impossible the monarch of Drury Lane could go out with any deputy whatever; and that, if he did, so far from his honour being vindicated, it would be more deeply involved.

"To this Elliston listened as to a perfectly new proposition, and fixing his eyes steadily on Lord William during a very lengthened pause—at last said—

"'But, my lord—there is one question yet.'

"'Name it, by all means.'

"'Might I suggest one more tumbler of brandy and water?'

"Lord William gave assent for a replenish of the glass, which the canteen man, having an eye to business, presently supplied.

"Elliston, having liberally tasted of this 'refresher,' committed himself to the confidence of another pause, after which he said—

"'And now, my lord, I would beg to ask, in which of the royal parks do you propose the meeting?'

"'Windsor, by all means,' replied the captain —'and what will be still more fitting, you shall fight under "Herne's Oak," and so make Shakespere himself one of the party.'

"Elliston gazed for a moment, perfectly overcome by the sublimity of the proposition, and then, with a very 'fargone' *impressement* of manner, exclaimed—

"'Herne's Oak! admirable! my lord—and my Lord Graham shall remember the words of Master Page, "There be many who do *fear* to walk by this Herne's Oak!"'—when up he rose.

"'Can I assist you, Elliston?' asked Lord William, offering him his cocked hat, and disentangling his sword from his silken legs.

"'By no means,' replied Elliston; 'but your man is a long time about *this* tumbler of brandy and water.'

"'Nay, nay,' cried Lord William, again laughing, 'you forget—you have already despatched it; and really, as it is very late——'

"'True, true!' interrupted Elliston, drawing out his watch, and looking at the reverse side of it; 'we must be going—Lord Graham will be punctual—hair triggers, my lord—and my hand is steady as iron.'

"'Hush! Do you know what day this is?—Sunday morning.'

"'Then,' said Elliston, 'your man is the more reprehensible in his delay of mixing this brandy and water.'

"After some further difficulty, the manager was placed in the hackney-coach. 'You'll follow, my lord?' said he, in a confidential whisper.

"'Certainly.'

"'Then, I am content. To Shooter's Hill!' exclaimed the manager to the coachman—and off he drove.

"The next morning, or rather that very morning, by ten o'clock, Robert William Elliston, in full possession of his energies, and far more alive to business than many about him, was at his writing-table."

In the course of the morning the following letter reached him :—

"Chamberlain's Office, May 3.

"Sir,—

"I regret to have heard that you felt hurt at some expression I used towards you last evening. This was far from my intention, my only object being to induce you to take some means which would remedy the disorder in the pit of the theatre; as well as the annoyance which it was to his Majesty, and the rest of the audience. I feel sorry that you should have misconceived me so as to suppose I would intentionally have said anything disagreeable to you.

"I remain, Sir, your obedient,

"GRAHAM."

It was after he had come to this sad complexion that he was so present to Charles Lamb, whose vivid sketch of him finds its illustration in the little stories just narrated.—" My acquaintance," he wrote, " with the pleasant creature whose loss we all deplore was but slight.

"But was he less *great* when in melancholy after-years, again, much near the same spot, I met him, when that sceptre had been wrested from his hand and his dominion was curtailed to the petty managership, and part-proprietorship, of the small Olympic, *his Elba?* He still played nightly upon the boards of Drury, but in parts, alas! allotted to him, not magnificently distributed by him. Waiving his great loss as nothing, and magnificently sinking the sense of fallen *material* grandeur in the more liberal resentment of depreciations done to his more lofty *intellectual* pretensions, ' Have you heard' (his customary exordium)—' have you heard,' said he, ' how they treat me? they put me in *comedy*.' Thought I—but his finger on his lips forbade any verbal interruption —' where could they have put you better?' Then, after a pause—' where I formerly played Romeo, I now play Mercutio,'—and so again he stalked away, neither staying, nor caring for, responses.

" O, it was a rich scene—but Sir Astley Cooper, the best of storytellers and surgeons, who mends a lame narrative almost as well as he sets a fracture, alone could do justice to it—that I was witness to, in the tarnished room (that had once been green) of that same little Olympic. There, after his deposition from imperial Drury, he substituted a throne. That Olympic Hill was his 'highest heaven;' himself, ' Jove in his chair.' There he sat in state, while before him, on complaint of the prompter, was brought for judgment —how shall I describe her?—one of those little tawdry things that flirt at the tails of choruses— a probationer for the town, in either of its senses —the pertest little drab—a dirty fringe and appendage of the lamps' smoke—who, it seems, on some disapprobation expressed by a ' a highly respectable' audience, had precipitately quitted her station on the boards, and withdrawn her small talents in disgust.

"'And how dare you,' said her manager—assuming a censorial severity which would have crushed the confidence of a Vestris, and disarmed that beautiful rebel herself of her professional caprices—I very believe, he thought *her* standing before him—'how dare you, madam, withdraw yourself, without a notice, from your theatrical duties?' 'I was hissed, sir.' 'And you have the presumption to decide upon the taste of the town?' 'I don't know that, sir, but I will never stand to be hissed,' was the subjoinder of young Confidence. When gathering up his features into one significant mass of wonder, pity, and expostulatory indignation—in a lesson never to have been lost upon a creature less forward than she who stood before him—his words were these: 'They have hissed *me.*'

"'Quite an Opera pit,' he said to me, as he was courteously conducting me over the benches of his Surrey Theatre, the last retreat, and recess of his every-day-waning grandeur.

"Those who knew Elliston, will know the *manner* in which he pronounced the latter sentence of the few words I am about to record. One proud day to me, he took his roast mutton with us in the Temple, to which I had superadded a preliminary haddock. After a rather plentiful partaking of the meagre banquet, not unrefreshed with the humbler sort of liquors, I made a sort of apology for the humility of the fare, observing that for my own part I never ate but one dish at dinner. 'I too never eat but one thing at dinner'—was his reply—then after a pause—'reckoning fish as nothing.' The manner was all. It was as if by one peremptory sentence he had decreed the annihiliation of all the savory esculents which the pleasant and nutritious food-giving Ocean pours forth upon poor humans from her watery bosom."

But the most quaint and farcical of his schemes was the opening of what he called a "Literary Association" at Bristol. What special twist in what Mr. Shandy would call his "pericraniacks" suggested this notion, it would be difficult to say: yet somehow it seems in harmony with his character. He might wish to stretch beyond his profession: to play the graceful *littérateur*, a part in which he felt that he could not hope to win credit otherwise than by professing it in this tangible shape. This institution which he thus grandly named was, in more sober phrase, a Circulating Library. The premises had been a pickle shop, which he recklessly purchased for the sum of £1600. The back parlour he styled THE LYCEUM, which he invited all that was refined and literary in Bristol to frequent, so as to acquire a "sweetness and light" that was sadly wanting to the commercial society of Bristol. This odd speculation was specially Ellistonian—no works of the ordinary pattern being admitted, the accomplished director laying out large sums in the purchase not merely of the old classical writers, but of black-letter volumes, so that the collection should be of a solid and important character. Antiquarian works of the profoundest sort—old travels of the early navigators—rare editions of English plays, were the inappropriate treasures secured for the heterogeneous collection: the collector we may be sure justifying each addition with flowing comments that must have been amusing to listen to. Not to neglect other departments of knowledge, he also gathered in a quantity of fossils, shells, Indian curiosities, arms, &c. (the invariable, but somewhat depressing, features of nearly every museum), and hung up with a sort of pleased triumph, the cynosure— a CHINESE GONG.—No wonder, it must be said again, that Charles Lamb was infinitely interested by such a character—which would have figured well in a comedy.

He was enthusiastic in the scheme, but, as might be expected, the back-parlour "Lyceum" remained empty. It was probably considered an eccentricity. It failed—a broken schoolmaster of the name of Orrick who was in charge, going off with such cash as there was in the concern. Yet with the airy projector, we may be certain it always remained a success—under the qualification that it had done all that he had intended, the seed being sown, &c. Indeed, he presently started another venture of the same kind at Leamington Spa, though, taught by experience, he conceded something to the practical spirit of business. A ragged collection of novels was got together, with which a meagre effort in the direction of stationery, &c., was combined. The whole was placed under the direction of his two sons. This sudden diversion —from the extreme æsthetic to sober prose and the concrete—was quite in keeping. Hither he would repair, as though to relax from greater cares, and even assist in the shop;—and, ever *acting*, thus offer to the Leamingtonian ladies the spectacle of one of his degree, and graceful bearing, stooping to such condescension. His first introduction to Lamb was upon this occasion. "E., whom nothing misbecame—to auspicate, I suppose, the filial concern, and set it going with a lustre—was serving in person two damsels fair, who had come into the shop, ostensibly to inquire for some new publication, but in reality to have a sight of the illustrious shopman, hoping some conference. With what an air did he reach down the volumes, dispassionately giving his opinion upon the work in question, and launching out into a dissertation on its comparative merits with those of certain publications of a similar stamp, its rival! his enchanted customers fairly hanging on his lips, subdued to the authoritative sentence. So have I seen a gentleman in comedy *acting* the shopman."

A pleasant *pendant* is Mr. Raymond's sketch of the elegant "shopman."

"One morning he descended early into his shop, and looking round with the irresistible humour of *Tangent* himself, 'It is my cruel fate,' said he, 'that my children will be gentlemen.' And, on his two sons making their appearance, they beheld their father, in an old dapple grey frock-coat, dusting the books, arranging the ink-bottles, re-piling the quires of 'Bath post,' and altering the position of the China mandarins, with the veriest gravity in the world. One of the first customers that came in was a short, dirty-faced drab of a maid-servant, who brought some books to be exchanged; and nearly at the same moment, a snivelling charity-boy, with a large patch of diachylon across his nose, placed himself at the counter, demanding other articles.

"'One at a time,' said *Octavian*, with petrifying solemnity. 'Now, madam?' pursued he, turning to the runt.

"'Missus a' sent back these here, and wants summut 'orrible.'

"'The lady's name?' demanded Elliston.

"'Wiwian,' grunted the girl.

"'With a V or a W?' asked Elliston with the same solemnity; but the wench only grinned; when up mounted *Sir Edward Mortimer* the ladder placed against his shelves, and withdrawing two wretchedly-torn volumes, clapped them together to liberate the dust, and placing them in the grubby claws of the now half-frightened girl—'There,' said he, 'a work of surpassing terror; and now, sir,' turning to the boy, 'I will attend to *you*.'

"The lad, who had by this time nearly pulled the plaster from his visage, owing to the nervous state of agitation into which he had been thrown, could not at the precise moment recollect his mission; when Elliston repeated with the intonation of a Merlin, 'And now, sir, I will attend to *you*.'

"'Half a quire of outsides and three ha'porth o' mixed wafers,' screamed the urchin, throwing fourpence-halfpenny on the counter.

"'Outsides,' repeated Elliston to his son William; 'mixed wafers,' said he in the same tone to Henry.

"*Doricourt* then demanded the paste-pot. Taking the brush, he first deliberately dabbed the lad's nose, thereby replacing the fallen diachylon; and then seizing a watering-pot, much to the merriment of a few strangers who were by this time collected about the shop, began sprinkling the steps of his library door. Having played a few further antics, the 'Great Lessee' retired to answer his numerous London correspondents on the stupendous affairs of Drury Lane."

To strangers, whom he wished to impress with the dignity of his position, his bearing seemed singular: but beneath it was a method and a meaning, though of a far-fetched, Ellistonian kind. Of this an odd illustration is recorded.

A gentleman of considerable merit as a Provincial actor once called by appointment at Drury Lane Theatre. He found Mr. Elliston, who had then the management, giving some directions on the stage, and was welcomed by him with great politeness. The manager, however, thinking, from the conversation which had passed, that the gentleman in question did not seem sufficiently impressed with the greatness of the person whom he was addressing, took this method of displaying his power and consequence. "Yes, sir," said Mr. Elliston, continuing the conversation previously commenced, with a slow and solemn enunciation, "the drama—is now—at its lowest ebb: and—" then suddenly breaking off, in a loud, emphatic voice he called, "First night watchman!" The man stepped forward, and making his bow, stood for orders. "And," resuming to the actor, "unless a material change—" again breaking off, he called —"Other night watchman!" with a peculiar emphasis. The call was obeyed as before—"a material change—I say—takes place—as Juvenal justly—Prompter!" The prompter came—"as Juvenal justly observes—Boxkeeper, dress circle, right hand! But, sir, a reaction must take place when—*Other* boxkeepers!" They came up—"Sir I say there must be a reaction—Copyist! Call-boy!"

Having collected all these personages about him without any apparent object, he turned to the actor, and saying in a slow magisterial tone, "Follow me," retired in a very dignified manner, leaving the minions of his power to guess what he wanted.*

But it is the Ellistonian advertisements that afford the richest entertainment. These are not to be classed with the artificial and vulgar allurements of the ordinary and conventional claptraps, in which their author has but small faith, save as a useful means of decoying the public. In Elliston's case, the charm is the perfect genuineness of these flourishes: he was addressing his public as he would address them from the stage: they were part of his "grand manner." He believed that these strange flourishings had a certain power: it was his fashion of working on those whom he addressed. Nothing too is more entertaining than the curious phrases, the strange inferences, and the abnormal English, not so much ignorance as the result of the grand and pompous confusion within. Thus are the mere prosaic elements, the object and aim of such advertisement, viz., the vulgar money objects, lifted into dignity by being connected with the loftiest associations. As when the

* 'Monthly Magazine.'

"Free list is suspended," not because of the crowds, &c., but lest the immortal Shakespeare "*should meet with opponents!*" A new piece cannot be produced on the day announced, and we hear the manager confidentially assuring his patrons, "that it must, in consequence of *an unexpected difficulty*, be postponed for a few days;" thus conveying a sense of mystery, of possibly secret influences at work, and asking for friendly confidence in himself.

It was when he took the reins at Drury Lane that he abandoned his grotesque advertisements and assumed this grand style. The centre of his play-bill,* which was the emphatic part of his communication, was printed in a flaming red type that contrasted effectively with the familiar rich black of the rest. This was his great official mode of communicating with his friends, and thus were conveyed meaning hints as to the future, suspicions, and, above all, lofty declarations of success. Thus, having secured Miss Wilson the vocalist, he assures the public in these red characters, "that *in* the determination to make the operatic company of this establishment superior *to*

---

* The Editor has gone over the vast collection of play-bills in the British Museum, with a view to a selection of some piquant passages. Nothing more entertaining can be conceived than the review of this strange gallery of eccentricity.

every former precedent, it is now with *equal pleasure and satisfaction* that the proprietor has to," &c. The young lady appeared; and Elliston on the following evening announced that " Miss Wilson made her first appearance yesterday evening, &c. The unbiassed opinion of the most brilliant, overflowing, and admiring audience that ever graced a Theatre Royal, and the enthusiastic fervour that accompanied the opera throughout, justifies the proprietor," in giving out the piece for repetition until further notice?—no—that was left to ordinary managers, but " in congratulating the musical world on this vast accession of talent, and to (sic) announce that," &c. A few days after he says that " the enthusiasm is beyond *every former precedent.* Not an order has been or will be given by the manager during Miss Wilson's engagement. The public decision has therefore been entirely unbiassed, and their admiration of the united talents engaged is confirmed by a demand for places, not exceeded by the most popular performances of the most prosperous period of this establishment."

Again, in red letters, a day or two later : " The enthusiasm which has been manifested," as before, &c. —" The general voice has decided upon her merits, and has demonstrated itself in applause of the most generous *and exhilarating fervour.* Not an order," &c., as before.

"P.S. Every seat in the Theatre was occupied before seven o'clock on Tuesday evening, and hundreds were disappointed in their desire to obtain a seat in the Boxes!"

Once more: "The opera continues its triumphant career. It is *an absolute fact* that at this moment there are more than THREE THOUSAND PLACES taken of Mr. Rodwell, the Box Bookkeeper," &c. Producing later a comedy and a melodrama, he says of the latter: "The new Melodrama is the most successful piece *that was ever produced!!!*" — It, however, had but moderate success. The Comedy he says, "was for the second time received with undiminished effect."—It would be the pride of the establishment "should the comedies of this Theatre be esteemed worthy of that *pre-eminent situation* the operatic company has attained."—One of his delightful forms of self-gratulation ran as follows: "and, without modestly adverting to the days of Garrick, the managers trust that their present and future efforts will, *without any temporary gasconade of the non-admission of orders,* be," &c.—This curious inversion is significant of the Elliston mind, and the "temporary gasconade" is specially charming.

Such faint qualifications of his lofty declarations were tributes reluctantly paid, *ex gratiâ*, to the conventional forms of society. They were indeed scarcely qualifications at all. Thus where the success of another piece had been decreed—for, as we have seen, the great man decided on this point, and even where a play had failed, gave judgment against the audience—he says it "met with a reception honourable to the industry, *as it is hoped*, of the establishment. It depended *on its best basis*, a powerful natural effect upon the feelings of the audience, and this is considered by the manager (*perhaps solely*) the best *medium to* the real patronage of the public." Here the "best basis," and "the medium to the real patronage," are admirable; but the placid qualification, "*perhaps solely*" would be most to the taste of a mind like Elia's.

But it was "The Coronation" that brought out all his eccentric power, and he literally revelled in the florid proclamations of that spectacle. It was given out that "*a fac-simile* of the real ceremonial was in preparation and would be announced in a few days, with a prefatory new comedy." Suddenly Edmund Kean appeared in England, and was secured as a fresh attraction by the clever Lessee.—

The Coronation would "keep," while the great tragedian was duly celebrated with the usual flourishing "red letters," most "tumultuous applause ever known," &c.—But the audience were kept in mind of the grand pageant that was preparing by sundry nods and whispers. The preparations were all the time "proceeding with the greatest activity, but as they have extended beyond the first intention, the theatre must be closed on Tuesday; and on Wednesday the Procession and all the paraphernalia, &c., will certainly," &c.—It was given out too that every one who had taken part in the real ceremony had been consulted.—When it was presented, "overflowing and delighted audiences nightly *recognise and acknowledge* the Coronation as the most correct and splendid exhibition ever," &c.

Hazlitt took issue on these rhodomontades, and boldly said that the theatre "did *not* overflow," and that the audiences were rather meagre. This was as nothing to our airy manager, who with his fanciful eye saw the vast crowds, mistily depicted, much as such a gathering is shadowed upon a "flat scene" on the modern stage. But his most ingeniously expressed pretext for not withdrawing it, to make place for one already announced, is well worthy being commemorated. The piece, he owned, had been promised, "but the demand for Boxes by families, *and a conviction that the complicated scenery employed* in this splendid exhibition *cannot, when once laid aside,* be replaced under a considerable time, has induced the manager," &c. Another show "being now *established* as the most gorgeous exhibition of scenic effect, *united with interest,* ever submitted to public opinion, it will be," &c.—Here should be marked by students of the grand, the parenthetic, careless way in which this panegyric is given,—i.e. "*being* now established;" "scenic effect united with interest" is a good touch: while a vulgar hand would have been content with "submitted to the public," instead of to "public opinion." How much, too, was insinuated by the description of a *piece* which, though received with "tumultuous approbation," had yet encountered hostility—a reception thus glanced at: "Every *factitious* (no doubt "factious") opposition previously organized being completely overpowered—the numerous communications on this subject that have been received *will, in due time, be brought before the public.*"

This sort of life did not last long. Dissipation altered his appearance, his figure and fine face showing fearful evidences of decay. All intelligence passed from that speaking face, and the elasticity of his step was gone.

It was at this very period that this most eccentric and extraordinary man contemplated two of the greatest projects of his life. Visionary and wild as they were, he yet followed them up for a time with an ardour which puzzled all physiological inquiry; a *second marriage* was the one, and a *seat in parliament* the other!

"His senatorial dream was a vision of no mean character. With the proceeds of 'Black-eyed Susan,' and the richer sum of his personal endowments, he purposed canvassing some western borough, and was actually in correspondence with parliamentary agents on the question. *Surrey*, certainly he had twice represented, and was still a sitting member; and had the franchise been extended at this time to the metropolitan boroughs, we are not quite clear how far his exertions might have led him towards success. The senatorial project, however, expired in the cradle of its birth—namely, the back-parlour of our hero in Blackfriars Road."

The marriage was an idea as eccentric—the object of his attentions being an elderly lady, oldest of three sisters, but who after all preliminaries were settled, declined to ally herself without bringing her two relatives into the family. A little later he was seized with apoplexy, and to the end maintained his character, "talking in a confused manner, and blessing his friends in the most placid and resigned manner."

On the 8th of July, 1831, he expired. Lamb wrote his epitaph—one of his happiest papers:—

"What new mysterious lodgings dost thou tenant now? or when may we expect thy aërial housewarming?

"Tartarus we know, and we have read of the Blessed Shades; now cannot I intelligibly fancy thee in either.

"There by the neighbouring moon mayst thou not still be acting thy managerial pranks, great disembodied Lessee? but still, and still a Manager.

"In Green-rooms, impervious to mortal eye, the muse beholds thee wielding posthumous empire.

"Thin ghosts of Figurantes (never plump on earth) circle thee in endlessly, and still their song is *Fye on sinful Fantasy*.

"Magnificent were thy capriccios on this globe of earth, ROBERT WILLIAM ELLISTON! for as yet we know not thy new name in heaven.

"It irks me to think, that, stript of thy regalities, thou shouldst ferry over, a poor forked shade, in crazy Stygian wherry. Methinks I hear the old boatman, paddling by the weedy wharf, with raucid voice, bawling 'SCULLS, SCULLS:' to which, with waving hand, and majestic action, thou deignest no reply, other than in two curt monosyllables, 'No : OARS.'

"But the laws of Pluto's kingdom know small difference between king and cobbler; manager and call-boy; and, if haply your dates of life were conterminant, you are quietly taking your passage, cheek by cheek (O ignoble levelling of Death), with the shade of some recently departed candle-snuffer."

CHAPTER VII.

GERALD GRIFFIN.*

During the last century it was a common incident in literary life, that a young man of "parts" and ability should be encouraged by the praises of his friends to put his poem or tragedy in his pocket, and set off, with some slender pittance, to try his fortune in London. Everything seemed rose-coloured, and the raptures of the village or country town critics might reasonably be looked for, if in less exuberant shape, from the more competent judges of the great metropolis. A certain amount of struggle and toil was to be expected: but this would be cheerfully undergone, and welcomed as a wholesome discipline.

The reality was very different, and there is a dismal uniformity in the story of such poor adventurers; who in a few very rare instances reached to favour, and to a competence, which the same amount of labour and purpose in another walk of life

* Born 1803, died 1840.

would have made a handsome fortune. But the great proportion, hopelessly committed to their task-work, sank into the condition of booksellers' hacks, and worked out their "time" in starvation or gin. These formed the great colony of Grub Street.

Still, just as the day labourer was nearly always secure of some wage, however miserable, so the hack might reckon on work of some description from the bookseller, on the usual "sweater's terms"—two guineas for a translated novel, and the like. But the playwriter's case might seem desperate. There were but two theatres open, rarely three: and the collection of Garrick's letters shows that the candidate playwriters included every class in the kingdom—clergymen, doctors, soldiers, clerks, shopmen, &c. It thus became a rueful sort of lottery.

This picture, it might be assumed, belonged to the past century, and the most interesting instance, of such a struggle is perhaps that of Goldsmith and his friend Johnson. Goldsmith's story, as told so gracefully by Mr. Forster, is almost painful; and it is with some relief that the reader thinks that the days of such miseries are passed away. It is remarkable, however, that within the days of our own generation this story should have been once more repeated, and with circumstances of an almost pathetic interest; and that a young fellow should have started from the banks of the Shannon with a half-written tragedy in his pocket, hoping by the aid of friends, but still more by the claims of his genius, to force booksellers, managers, and actors to give him a hearing. The progress of this illusion, its gradual fading out under the miserable logic of privation, and the clinging to hope, the cheerfulness assumed for the sake of those at home, who were finding the small pittance with which he could hardly keep body and soul together in the world of London, make up the touching story of Gerald Griffin, told best in his own words.

Before he was twenty he found himself in London with an unfinished tragedy, and one friend, on whom all his hopes rested. This was in the year 1823, and the tale of his troubles is shown in a series of letters to his family.

"My Dear William," he writes, full of enthusiasm, "I have just had rather a long interview with —— at his house, and he has kept the tragedy of 'Aguire' for the purpose of reading it. He asked me what the plot, &c., of the piece was, and promised to give me an answer in the course of next week if possible; at least he said I might depend on the earliest he could give. You may remember some time before I left Ireland, I told you the plot of a tragedy which I at first intended to be called 'The Prodigal Son,' —— (an actor) tells me that it is the name of the new tragedy which Banim has presented, and which has been accepted at Drury Lane. He says he will give me an answer next week; otherwise he cannot promise so soon, so that until then, I can enjoy all the delights of suspense in their fullest force. Every one to whom I showed the play here assured me of its success; among the rest your old friend Mr. W—. I have had a tiresome piece of work since I came, transcribing the play, which I was told was almost illegible. With respect to the situation of reporter it is almost impossible to procure it at present, as the business season has not commenced. That of police reporter is easy enough I believe to be procured, but I am told the office is scarcely reputable. I shall take a report of some matter, and send it to the papers the first opportunity. I have had such harassing work looking after addresses, &c., together with continued writing, and the terrible damp fogs that have prevailed here lately, that I got this week a renewal of my old attacks of chest.

I am however, much better. With respect to the state of my finances, they are getting low. I was put to some expense while looking for lodgings, as my good friend P— had no bed. If you could spare me a few pounds, I am pretty certain I can do something shortly. At all events write to me, and let me know what you think of my prospects and of what I have done and ought to do."

"MY DEAR WILLIAM," he again wrote, on Nov. 22, 1823. "I never experienced until this morning what the pain was of receiving unpleasant news from home. The account which you give of the state of your health was as unexpected as it was distressing. The bill on Sir E. Flyn and Co. I have received. It was entirely too much for you to send me under the circumstances. Half the money would I am sure with economy enable me to get through until I have procured a way of doing something. I have sent some pieces to the New Monthly Magazine, and if they are accepted I intend to offer Colburn the first number of a series of papers. He pays liberally for these contributions. The success of this however, I do not set much reliance upon. I intend to report the trial of the murderers of Weare, which will come on soon. I am not so sanguine about my prospects as that I could not easily resign myself to a disappointment. Mr. W— often advises me to avoid it, as he says there are so many mortifications mingled even with success, that a person who is very sanguine is sure to be disappointed. But among all the dampers I meet, there is not such a finished croaker as a young student at the bar, who is himself a disappointed dramatist, and never meets me without some agreeable foreboding or other With respect to the taste of a London audience, you may judge what it is, when I tell you that 'Venice Preserved' will scarcely draw a decent house; while such a piece of unmeaning absurdity as the 'Cataract of the Ganges' has filled Drury Lane every night these three weeks past. The scenery and decorations, field of battle, burning forest, and cataract of real water, afforded a succession of splendour I had no conception of, but I was heartily tired of the eternal galloping, burning; marching, and counter marching, and the dull speechifying with which it abounds. A lady on horseback riding up a cataract is rather a bold stroke, but these things are quite the rage now. They are hissed by the gods, but that is a trifle so long as they fill the house and the manager's pockets. I build great hopes out of the burning convent and the thunder storm, if 'Aguire' should be accepted, as well as a grand procession and chorus which I have introduced in the second act. My dearest William, I hope your next letter will bring me better accounts than that which now lies before me. I have set my happiness if I should succeed, on sharing with you the pleasures and pains of authorship, and if this unfortunate attack should disable you (though I have fervent hopes it may not turn out so serious as you fear,) greater success than I can ever hope for would make no amends. Your affectionate and grateful, GERALD GRIFFIN."

"MY DEAR WILLIAM," he wrote on Dec. 29, 1823, "I mentioned to you a few days since, that I had seen Banim. I dined with him on Thursday; there were Mrs. Banim and an Irish gentleman, and we had a pleasant evening enough. He had read 'Aguire' twice. He went over it scene by scene with me, and pointed out all the passages he disliked. He then gave me his candid opinion, which was, that after making those alterations, the play ought to be accepted, and to succeed. He gave it very high praise indeed, especially the third and fourth acts, which he said could not be better. Parts of the others he found fault with

The piece would not suffer by the loss of those passages, as he thought the acts too long. He recommended me to persevere in writing for the stage, and if I did so, to foreswear roses, dewdrops, and sunbeams for ever. The fate of the unfortunate 'Vespers of Palermo' told me this before. Poetry is not listened to on the stage here. I could not on the whole, have expected Banim to act a more friendly or generous part than he has done. On the second day I called on him (Saturday), he made me stop to dinner. I put the direct question to him, whether from what he had seen it was his real opinion that I should be successful as a dramatist. His reply was, that he thought I had every claim, and since I had dealt so candidly with him, he advised me to write on, and that he would do everything for any piece I wished to bring forward, that he would do if it was his own. With respect to the present piece, he advised me to leave it in ——'s hands until he sends it to me and not call or write to him. If he knows anything of him, he says he will keep and play it. I am very sorry I did not see Banim first. In that case I should long since have known its fate, as he could have procured me an answer from the committee in ten days. I have not been able to procure an engagement since I wrote last. It is very difficult to do so. I intend however to make a desperate effort this week, for it must be done before long or not at all. I have got a cold and an ugly cough at present, but my health on the whole is very tolerable. I have been obliged to lay out nearly half the money you sent me, in clothes, as without them I might as well have remained at home. I owe but the last week for my lodgings, but if I cannot get an engagement very shortly, I will give them up altogether, for the rent is too much for me."

Thus far all promised fairly, but the slow and cruel process of *désillusionnement* was now to begin. The little salves and excuses he finds for this check are almost piteous.

In January 1824 he wrote:—

"MY DEAR WILLIAM, —— has sent me back my piece (I don't like that word rejected,) after keeping it nearly three months, without any opinion, other than the mere act of doing so. I had just the day before said to Banim, that I wished he would do it, for I heartily disliked the idea of his being considered my patron if he should accept it. From the description I have received of the manner in which actors deal with those who are brought before the public through their instrumentality, I am in a fine vein for cutting at them. Pope says very truly, they are judges of what is good just as a tailor is of what is graceful. Johnson, that sensible old fellow, always despised them. The fact was of all the introductions I could get, none could have been slighter than that I handed to ——, though I thought it a fine thing at the time. Of all the people I could have applied to, an actor was the least likely to pay me attention; and of all actors I could have selected, —— was the worst: for, you must know he dabbles in tragedy himself; and I suppose you recollect the whisper to Sir Fretful or Puff, (which is it?) in the 'Critic,'—'Never send a piece to Drury'—'Writes himself?' 'I know it, sir.' However, after all this, the piece deserved to be rejected, for it had many and grevious sins. Banim said if I change the name and make those alterations he pointed out, he will present it for me and get me an immediate answer. With a true, indefatigible, Grub Street spirit, I have commenced a new one and have it nearly finished . . . . There is a great dearth of talent in that way at present. You were right in supposing that there are a great number of pieces presented at the theatres. Banim tells me he supposes there are no less than a thousand rejected every year. I was born under some extraordinary planet I believe. You recollect the coincidences I before mentioned to you. A tragedy founded on the story of Aguire and called the Spanish Revenge, has been presented at Covent Garden and rejected. . . . . I have been very busy lately, both in writing and endeavouring to procure some regular employment. . . . GERALD GRIFFIN."

Another month and there is a further descent:—

"Feb. 1824. Since I last wrote, I have been making the utmost efforts to secure some immediate way of support, and nevertheless, in that point, still remain in abeyance. Banim, who is very kind to me, can do nothing at present with the press, as those with whom he has influence are all pre-occupied. Of the daily or political press he knows nothing. On my calling on him, I believe the day after I wrote to you last, he urged me to alter Aguire, in those passages he pointed out, and told me that he still persevered in his opinion of it: that there were scenes in it which for stage effect and every requisite could not be better. I have conned the play over so often myself, that I don't know what's bad or good in it but as I am told, and therefore found the alterations very troublesome.

"I trust in God that I may be enabled to do something which will prevent my again trespassing on you. I could not economize more rigidly than I do. My lodgings I have still kept, as at that time I owed a little, and if I was to go into new, I should be obliged to pay ready money for some time, and that is not now absolutely necessary where I am; and considering the difference in charge I could procure another for, the advantage I think was on the side of the remaining. I have now shewn you my circumstances. Before another fortnight or three weeks, I think I shall be able to let you know that I have been either accepted or rejected at the theatres. I find —— has been with you. He left this I believe the very day I received my manuscript. Peace be with him! he has cured me of histrionic patrons."

His distresses were now slowly gathering, and his hopes sinking in the same measure.

In March, he wrote:—

"I must have heartily tired and sickened you before now, and I am sick and tired myself. I had little idea before I left Ireland that it was possible I could be nearly five months in London without doing anything; but it is not through my remissness that has been the case. A very little time longer will tell me all that I have to expect, and I shall then take measures accordingly. I had a visit from Banim the other day. What with the delays and disappointments I have met since I came here, it is only his encouragement, and his friendship that keeps hope alive. I shall write to you again when I know the issue of the play, which I have long since finished."

". . . . Banim's friendship I find every day growing more ardent, more cordial if possible. I dined with him on Sunday last. I told you in my last, I had left him four acts of a play, for the purpose of leaving it to his option, to present that or Aguire, I anticipated the preference of the new, and have with him succeeded to my wish. He says it is the best I have written yet, and will be when finished 'a most effective play!' but what gives me the greatest satisfaction respecting it, is the consciousness that I have written an original play. That passion of revenge you know was threadbare. Banim has made some suggestions which I have adopted. I will finish it immediately, place it in his hands, and abide the result in following other pursuits. He advises me to have it presented at Covent Garden, for many reasons. Imprimis they are more liberal; next Gisippus is a character for Young or Macready; the former I should rather to undertake it, as I have placed the effect of the piece more in pathos than violent passion. He wishes to speak to Young, who is his intimate friend, before he presents it, in order to learn all the Green Room secrets. Young will be in town this week. Banim made me an offer the other day, which will be of more immediate advantage than the tragedy, inasmuch as I need not abide the result. He desired me to write a piece for the English Opera House. When I have it finished he will introduce me to Mr. Arnold of Golden Square, the proprietor, who is his friend, and get me immediate money for it without awaiting its performance. This was exactly such an offer as I wanted, and you may be sure I will avail myself of it. It is doubly advantageous as the English Opera House continues open until next winter, but I must see it first. You see our prospects go on slowly, but every day I feel the ground more firm beneath my feet. Banim offers me many introductions. He is acquainted with Thomas Moore—who was to see him the other day—Campbell and others of celebrity. The less I think that is said about my theatrical views at present the better. O Lord! if I should be damned after all this! But no! that will not be the case I am sure, for I have a presentiment of success. What would I have done if I had not found Banim? I should have instantly despaired on ——'s treatment of me. I should never be tired of talking about and thinking of Banim. Mark me, he is a man. The only one I have met since I have left Ireland, almost."

Again, on March 31st:—

"MY DEAREST ELLEN.—It is now a long time since I have written to, or heard directly from Pallas. William mentioned in his last that you were very ill, but I hope you do not add to your already severe sufferings those of imagination: indeed I know you do not. Oh! my dear Ellen, if I could but transfer to you and William a little of the hope—the bright expectancy that cheers and buoys up my own spirit through the anxiety of suspense, I think it would be well both for your health and happiness. I am not impatient, though anxious. *I should myself have wondered if I had struck at once into reputation and independence.* ——'*s rejection of me, I regard as a dispensation of Providence.* I was a *leetle* too confident perhaps, and it was a seasonable humiliation in the commencement of my career. However this does not excuse him. I do not say he might not have rejected me, but his manner of doing so was bad. He knew I was a stranger in London, young and inexperienced in such matters, and his countryman, and he kept me in suspense three months; then sent back my piece without comment, wrapped in an old paper, and unsealed! If I had any wish for a little revenge —but I have not—I understand it will soon be gratified in some measure. The affair, without mentioning names, will be taken up in one of Blackwood's forthcoming magazines—not much to his advantage. I have no enmity to the man, but for justice' sake, I don't grudge him whatever he gets from Blackwood for it."

There could be nothing more painfully interesting to a student of human nature than the fitful turns and changes in this poor adventurer. Under these many rallies an affected buoyancy can be found, with the sinking of despair; and the passage in italics offers an exquisite stroke of character. Two months more, and such attempts at veiling the hideous truth from himself were abandoned. In May he wrote:—

" For myself, I am quite tired of this, if I may

use a *cockney* idiom, *hot water* kind of life; or our own more rich and expressive mode of conveying the idea, ' pulling the devil by the tail.' It would be a great thing for me, if I could secure a present livelihood, while I prosecuted other views at the same time, for I cannot do anything with confidence or ease, while I have the terrible idea starting on my mind at intervals that it *may* possibly be that I am mispending time; but this at least I hope is not the case. At all events there are many things I could then do, which I can scarcely do now with comfort; among the rest, writing for magazines, which I have been strongly recommended to try, and which one gentleman whom I know, told me he used to make £300 a year by, and yet without permanently engaging himself with any. Of the great theatres I know I cannot form any immediate expectation. And the summer one is not open yet.

"I will tell you now some things which will give you some idea of the drama, and the dramatic management of the day, which however for the credit of the *métier*, I would not breathe to ' ears profane.' Of all the walks in literature, it certainly is at present the most heart-rending, the most toilsome, and the most harassing to a man who is possessed of a mind that may be at all wrought on by circumstances. The managers only seek to fill their houses, and don't care a curse for all the dramatists that ever lived. . . Literary men see the trouble which attends it, the bending and cringing to performers, the chicanery of managers, and the anxiety of suspense, which no previous success can relieve them from—and therefore it is that they seek to make a talent for some other walk, and content themselves with the quiet fame of a 'closet writer,' which is accompanied with little or none of the uneasiness of mind which the former brings with it. . . . For us, poor devils—who love the drama well, and are not so confident in other branches of that most toilsome and thankless of all professions, authorship—we must only be content to wade through thick and thin, and make our goal as soon as we may. This saw-dust and water work will pass away like everything else, and then perchance the poor half-drowned muse of the buskin may be permitted to lift her head above the flood once more. I don't know how it is, though I have never put a line in print since I came here—at least so that I was known in it by anybody—I have got a sneaking kind of reputation as a poet among my acquaintances.

"With regard to comedy, the surest ground for a comic writer to go on, is to select present manners, follies, and fashions for his target. These *hits* always *tell* well in the performance, and carry off many a heavy plot. Croly has practised this with success in his piece. Shall I tell you a secret? *The most successful dramatist of our day, I mean as to the number of successful pieces he produced, wrote six plays before he could get one accepted.*"

Later he wrote to his sister:—

"Do you know I cannot help thinking sometimes, that we should all have been better and happier if we had accompanied the first emigrants of our family and settled with them in Susquehana. For my part, situated as I am at present, uncertain of the ground I stand on, and sickened by repeated delays and disappointments, there is only one thing that makes me imagine I should not be more at ease there, and that is that I know I never could be so anywhere, until I had tried London; and even yet, nothing but the consideration of being amongst my friends would induce me to make the exchange: I mean to say being amongst them, and seeing them in health and comfort. I look on success now as a matter of mere business and nothing more. As to fame, if I could accomplish it in any way, I should scarcely try for its sake alone. I believe it is the case with almost everybody before they succeed, to wear away all relish for it in the exertion. I have seen enough of literature and literary men to know what it is, and I feel convinced, that at the best, and with the highest reputation, a man might make himself as happy in other walks of life. I see those who have got it as indifferent about it as if totally unknown, while at the same time they like to add to it. But money! money is the grand object—the all in all. I am not avaricious, but I see that they are the happiest who are making the most, and am so convinced of the reality of its blessings, that if I could make a fortune by *splitting matches*, I think I never would put a word in print."

Again:—

"My employment, I mean that which procured me immediate remuneration, has for the present ceased. I have something yet on hands, but though the bookseller who suggested the idea to me promised to engage in it, he would not speak of terms until it is completed. This will not be before six or seven weeks, and though certain of disposing of it after that time, mere *hope* will not lend me her wings to fly over the interval. You may judge what a mercenary scribbler I am, and how unwilling to let a job slip through my fingers, when I tell you that I engaged to translate, and actually translated a volume and a half of one of Prevot's works, for two guineas! My dear Dan, tell this not in Gath; publish it not in the streets of Askalon."

His next bitter revelation, though gaily made, is significant.

"Under such circumstances as these, it is rather vexatious that I cannot avail myself of my own exertions through such a mortifying and apparently trivial obstacle as the state of my *garde-robe*. Banim has been with me twice within the last fortnight; first to tell me that Dr. Maginn, who is the principal writer in Blackwood, had very kindly offered, without any personal knowledge of me, to introduce me to the 'editor of the Literary Gazette,' (his intimate friend,) and the second time to ask me to dine at his house with some literary gentlemen, amongst whom was Dr. Maginn.

Both invitations I was obliged to decline, (on the score of being closely occupied,) and the next morning Banim called again at my lodgings, and not finding me at home, left a note to say that he was sorry I did not come, but whenever I chose he would feel great pleasure in introducing me to those gentlemen, who were anxious for my acquaintance. With the assistance of heaven, I hope I shall after some time be enabled to get over this difficulty." Again he says: "It will be necessary for me now in order to procure more drudgery, to go out among the publishers; this I cannot do, because of the prevention I have mentioned. The fact is, I am at present almost a complete prisoner; I wait until dusk every evening, to creep from my mouse-hole, and snatch a little fresh air on the bridge close by. Good heaven! to think that I am here in the centre of mountains of wealth; almost 'upon 'Change,' and to have no opportunity of laying an *honest* hand upon a stray draft in its flight from one commercial fellow to another, who has no more business with it than I have with—anything that I have too much of already and don't know what to do with—say common sense and modesty."

"You have no idea what a heart-breaking life

that of a young scribbler beating about, and endeavouring to make his way in London is; going into a bookseller's shop, as I have often done, and being obliged to praise up my own manuscript, to induce him to look at it at all—for there is so much competition, that a person without a name will not even get a trial—while he puts on his spectacles, and answers all your self-commendation with a 'hum—um;'—a set of hardened villains! and yet at no time whatever could I have been prevailed upon to quit London altogether. That horrid word failure,—No!—death first! There is a great tragic actress here who offered to present my play, and do all in her power to have it acted, but I have been sickened of such matters for a little while. I may however set about it some other time. Why I have yesterday written a play (in one act) which is to be published this week with a most laughable illustration by the Hogarth of the day, George Cruikshank. There's dramatic fame for you! In blank verse too, mind I don't say poetry! I have a conscience as well as another man."

Friends, even his dearest one Banim, noticed that he shunned their company, and grew morbidly sensitive and reserved. One went in search of him, and after much difficulty discovered him in a poor district, in a squalid lodging, the landlady of which expressed her fears that he was in want of the necessaries of life, and was besides battling against illness. An offer of assistance was made, which was rejected haughtily, and resentfully, by the poor struggler. Precisely at this moment, when the strain had became unendurable, these gallant efforts found some reward: and this darkest hour proved to be the last before the dawn, or some good promise of the dawn. Then, and then only, did the unselfish creature open his heart to those at home, and ask sympathy for what he had gone through.

Nearly two years of this terrible struggle had gone by, and he thus at last confided to his parents all he had suffered:—

"My dear, ever dear Father and Mother,—Under the circumstances as they appear to you, it is matter more of pain than astonishment to me, that you should have been so entirely at a loss in finding excusable motives for my silence. It is one of those misfortunes (and I hope the last of them) which the miserable and galling life I have led since I came to London (until very lately) has thrown on my shoulders, and which of course I must endure as well as I can. But if you knew, my dear Mother, what that life has been, it would I believe have led you to a less injurious conclusion to me. Until within a short time back I have not had since I left Ireland a single moment's peace of mind—constantly—constantly running backward and forward and trying a thousand expedients, and only to meet disappointments everywhere I turned. It may perhaps appear strange and unaccountable to you, but I could not sit down to tell you only that I was in despair of ever being able to do anything in London, as was the fact for a long time. I never will think or talk upon the subject again. It was a year such as I did not think it possible I could have outlived, and the very recollection of it puts me into the horrors. Let me first, however, beg you to be satisfied that this it was, and no neglect—I was not guilty of it for an instant—that prevented my writing; beside that when I do write I must fill up a large sheet, or send none. When first I came to London, my own self-conceit, backed by the opinion of one of the most original geniuses of the age, induced me to set about revolutionizing the dramatic taste of the time by writing for the stage. Indeed the design was formed, and the first step taken (a couple of pieces written) in Ireland. I cannot with my present experience conceive anything more comical than my own views and measures at the time. A young gentleman totally unknown, even to a single family in London, coming into town with a few pounds in one pocket, and a brace of tragedies in the other, supposing that the one will set him up before the others are exhausted, is not a very novel, but a very laughable delusion. 'Twould weary you, or I would carry you through a number of curious scenes into which it led me. Only imagine the modest young Munsterman spouting his tragedy to a room full of literary ladies and gentlemen; some of high consideration too. The applause however of that circle on that night was sweeter, far sweeter to me, than would be the bravos of a whole theatre at present, being united at the time to the confident anticipation of it. One of the people present immediately got me an introduction to —— (I was offered several for all the actors). To —— I went—and he let down the pegs that made my music. He was very polite—talked and chatted about himself and Shiel and my friend—excellent friend Banim. He kept my play four months, wrote me some nonsensical apologies about keeping it so long, and *cut* off to Ireland, leaving orders to have it sent to my lodgings, without any opinion. I was quite surprised at this, and the more so, as Banim, who is one of the most successful dramatic writers, told me he was sure he would keep it: at the same time saying, what indeed I found every person who had the least theatrical knowledge join in, that I acted most unwisely in putting a play into an actor's hands. But enough of theatricals? Well, this disappointment sent me into the contrary extreme. I before imagined I could do anything; I now thought I could do nothing. One supposition was just as foolish as the other. It was then I set about writing for those weekly publications; all of which, except the 'Literary Gazette,' cheated me abominably. Then finding this to be the case, I wrote for the great magazines. My articles were generally inserted; but on calling for payment—seeing that I was a poor inexperienced devil, there was so much shuffling and shabby work that it disgusted me, and I gave up the idea of making money that way. I now lost heart for everything; got into the cheapest lodgings I could make out, and there worked on, rather to divert my mind from the horrible gloom that I felt growing on me in spite of myself, than with any hope of being remunerated.

This, and the recollection of the expense I had put William to, and the fears—that every moment became conviction—that I should never be enabled to fulfil his hopes or my own expectations, all came pressing together upon my mind and made me miserable. A thousand, and a thousand times I wished that I could lie down quietly and die at once, and be forgotten for ever. But that however was not to be had for the asking. I don't think I left anything undone that could have changed the course of affairs, or brought me a little portion of the good luck that was going on about me; but good luck was too busy elsewhere. I can hardly describe to you the state of mind I was in at this time. It was not an indolent despondency, for I was working hard, and I am now—and it is only now—receiving money for the labour of those dreadful hours. I used not to see a face that I knew, and after sitting writing all day, when I walked in the streets in the evening it actually seemed to me as if I was of a different species altogether from the people about me. The fact was, from pure anxiety alone I was more than half dead, and would most certainly have given up the ghost I believe, were it not that by the merest accident on earth, the literary friend who had procured me the unfortunate introduction a year before dropped in one evening to 'have a talk' with me. I had not seen him, nor anybody else that I knew, for some months, and he frightened me by saying I looked like a ghost. In a few days however a publisher of his acquaintance had got some things to do—works to arrange, regulate, and revise; so he asked me if I would devote a few hours in the middle of every day to the purpose for £50 a year. I did so, and among other things which I got to revise was a weekly fashionable journal. After I had read this for some weeks, I said to myself, 'Why hang it, I am sure I can write better than this at any rate.' And at the same time I knew that the contributors were well paid. I wrote some sketches of London life, and sent them anonymously to the editor, offering to contribute without payment. . . . . I have the satisfaction to see my articles quoted and commended in the daily papers; satisfaction, I say, as everything of that kind gives me a firmer hold of the paper. The theatrical department is left altogether to me; and I mortify my revengeful spirit by invariably giving —— (the actor) all the applause he could expect, or in justice lay claim to. I assure you I feel a philosophical pride and comfort in thus proving to myself that my conduct is not to be influenced by that of another, no matter how nearly the latter may affect my interests. Thus, things begin to look in smiles upon me at last. I have within the past fortnight cleared away the last of the debts I had incurred here with the good fortune of meeting them in full time to prevent even a murmur. With the assistance of heaven, I hope my actual embarrassments ('tis laughable to apply the words to such little matters as they are) have passed away for ever.—Your affectionate son, "GERALD GRIFFIN."

Had passed away for ever! It happily proved that he spoke with certainty. With this the tide began to turn in the most remarkable way; he discovered a vein for story-telling, and the charming 'Collegians'—a tale written with much of the grace of his countryman Goldsmith—was presently to make his name known, and raise him above want. Then followed success and reputation.

Mr. Forster, with the sympathy of a man of genius, has admirably touched the true significance of this story—which has been too long overlooked:—

"Gerald Griffin's life was one of those strange, silent romances which pass quite unheeded amid the roar and movement of the busier life around them; yet the reader will find a brief mention of it not at all inappropriate to my present subject. He was a Limerick man, and at the age of twenty, eager to make a great dash upon the stage, he came up to London without a friend, but with one tragedy finished in his pocket, and another rapidly forming in his brain. The desperate craving of his youth was to force his way into the London theatres, and he seems to have determined very resolutely to use the faculty of which he felt himself possessed to that end, failure or neglect to the contrary notwithstanding—*Aguire*, his first tragedy, making no way towards a hearing, he wrote a second. This was *Gisippus*, and written as it was in his twentieth year, I do not hesitate to call it one of the marvels of youthful production in literature. The solid grasp of character, the manly depth of thought, the beauties as well as defects of the composition (more than I can here enumerate), wanted only right direction to have given to our English drama another splendid and enduring name. In little London coffee-houses, on little strips of paper, the tragedy was written. But he could get no hearing for it. Still undaunted, he wrote a comedy, he wrote farces—he tried the stage at every avenue, and it would have none of him. Meanwhile, he had been starving for two miserable years; waiting all day within doors, and never venturing out till darkness threw its friendly veil over his threadbare coat; to use the common phrase, *denying himself* (because he could not get them) the common necessaries of life; fasting 'three days together without tasting food,' in a small room in an obscure court near St. Paul's; living for the most part, in short, on such munificent booksellers' rewards as two guineas for the translation of a volume and a half of a French novel. Something better presented itself at last however, and emerging from his misery, he became a critic, a reporter, and, stimulated by Banim's success, a writer of Irish tales. His dramatic dream was dreamt, and he never returned to the stage again. But not without ill effects to himself could he hope to keep thus dormant and unused the faculty which, as it seems to me, he had received in greatest abundance. More even than the zeal of God's House, in his later years this *eat him up*."

He had bade adieu for ever to what had at first tempted him to London—the delicious *ignis fatuus* of the stage, which had led him on through so many miseries. His poetical plays were flung aside and never thought of again.—Suddenly, in the midst of his success, not under the pressure of any wretchedness, the thought occurred to him that there was something more worthy of his energies, and of the purpose of a life, than the writing popular stories for bread; and, without ostentation or parade of piety, he quietly withdrew himself from the world and retired to a monastery, where he lived a happy life, then fell into a sudden fever, and died holily. Before entering the monastery he had burnt his first play 'Aguire'—but had stayed his hand when he came to 'Gisippus,' " perhaps," as Mr. Forster says, " in touching memory of his early hopes, and that some record might be left in vindication of them." Two years after his death came the ironical *amende* of fortune: not however too late; for the author, had he been alive, would probably have been indifferent. The piece was taken from the dusty shelf or forgotten drawer, brought out at Drury Lane, adorned with the splendid acting of Macready and Miss Faucit, and received triumphantly. The Press exhausted itself in praises. As the curtain fell the audience rose to their feet, and the theatre rang with acclamations. It was felt that a work full of grace and beauty had been presented. The great actress, and the greater actor, who had interpreted the chief characters, were summoned again and again. Nor was this the conventional tribute, that has since become hackneyed. The piece grew in popularity, and was acted many times. Yet it was owned that, mixed with the triumph there was a sort of painful feeling—an indistinct sense that the recognition had been delayed too long—until the now-acclaimed author was in his grave. Few, however, knew the story of the struggle, the agonies of hope and suffering, connected with they piece the witnessed. Fewer still knew that the author had closed his weary life, a poor simple monk, and was now at rest by the waters of the River Lee.

There is no such affecting chapter in the whole pathetic chronicle of the Stage.

CHAPTER VIII.

THE YOUNG ROSCIUS.
1791.

WERE it announced, during the present year, that there was still living a person who had been the talk of the whole kingdom, and a popular idol, fully seventy years ago, such a statement might fairly be received with wonder or incredulity. Such a phenomenon involves a union of longevity and of distinction not likely to be found in the same person. Yet Mr. or "Master" Betty, once the "Young Roscius," who died in the month of August in the present year, was transporting vast audiences with delight, was sought and run after, in the year 1803, and may be thus considered the single celebrity of that era who has survived to our day. Further, he stands at the head of the line of "infant prodigies," if, indeed, he may not be distinguished from that uninteresting class. It seems to be understood that there was something singularly attractive, and that touched the heart, in the performance of "this beautiful and intelligent boy," as he was called—a something that enabled him to surmount the awkward incongruities of his theatrical position, such as the spectacle of a child acting with grown-up people. It was a very original and striking performance, distinguished from the feeble and unpleasant efforts of other infant performers. Much that is interesting and even romantic belongs therefore to the story of "young Master Betty," who so lately departed as the very old Mr. Betty.

Dr. Betty, an Irish doctor from the north of Ireland, had married an English lady named Stanton, who was of genteel family. Later, this point was much insisted on, and all connection with the stage disclaimed, for certain malicious persons insinuated that Stanton was a name well known in the profession; as indeed readers of Boswell will recollect, a Lichfield manager of that name having waited on Dr. Johnson to ask him to command a play. She, it seems, brought to her husband the handsome but oddly-named "manor of Hopton Wafers," while he himself possessed a competence. They were staying at Shrewsbury when the prodigy "Master Henry Betty" was born, an event which took place on

Sept. 13th, 1791, and was duly registered at St. Chad's Church. When he was five years old, the whole family returned to the north of Ireland, where Mr. Betty embarked in what was grandly described as " business relating to the linen manufacture near Ballynahinch," combining with it a little farming. Here the boy was duly educated, his genteel mother paying particular attention to his pronunciation and accent, " as they were living in a district where the English tongue was spoken in its worst depravity." One day the child heard his father declaim Wolsey's speech, and on asking what was the meaning of the gestures, was told they were what is usually styled acting. " What great events," says the deeply-impressed chronicler of Master Betty's career, " spring from events apparently trivial! From this moment, it seems, his destiny was determined!" The boy began to learn speeches out of plays, which he used to recite on the sideboard for friends. The passion grew in him, until some of the genteel relations in England heard of his taste, and interposing, required that it should be summarily checked.

It came to pass, however, that in the year 1802 the great Siddons was playing in Belfast, and

Master Betty was taken to see her in Elvira. He was enchanted. "When he returned home, he told his father, with a look of such enthusiasm, and a voice so pathetic that those who heard him will never forget the expression, that he should certainly die if he was not to be a player." He could think of nothing but the divine Elvira; he learned her speeches, and became so possessed with theatrical ideas that his father took him to the Belfast manager, Atkins, and made him recite before him. Mr. Hough, the prompter, a man of more practical mind, was next called in to give his advice—was invited on a visit to the Bettys' house, where he gave the boy instruction. It is quite evident therefore that the genteel Bettys, from the beginning, were not disinclined to turn their child's talents to profit, though they affected to give out that they were driven to allow what they disapproved. As at this time the rebellion was going on, all the theatres were shut; but when matters were more composed, an arrangement was made with Atkins—"a man of friendly disposition and character"—for the boy's appearance at his theatre. The first appearance of the prodigy was announced for August 16th, 1803, in execrable grammar that sufficiently corresponded with "the worst depravity of pronunciation" that obtained in the district. "Mr. Atkins presents his respects to the ladies and gentlemen of Belfast, *and the public*, that, willing to bring forward every novelty in his power, he has, through the intercession of several ladies, prevailed on the friends of a young gentleman only eleven years old, whose theatrical abilities have been the wonder and admiration of all who have heard him, *to* perform in public two or three of the characters he most excels in." 'Zara' was the piece selected, from the pen of " that ingenious author Voltaire." Martial law was still in force, and the theatre had to be closed by nine o'clock; but to oblige the manager, "the drums had been ordered to beat an hour later than usual." Every one in Belfast, of course, knew it was "little Betty" that was coming forward, and the curiosity was extraordinary. The success was stupendous, and the applause tumultuous. The boy (whose age was truthfully announced, though, according to professional usage, he might fairly have been introduced as being only eight years old) played with extraordinary feeling and composure. Next day the whole town was talking of the performance. The hardheaded flax-spinners of the town were sceptical, but went to judge for themselves. His fame spread to Dublin, and Jones, the well-known manager, to whom Mr. Croker addressed his 'Familiar Epistles,' at once made an engagement with him. On November 28th 'Douglas' was announced, the part of Norval "by a young gentleman only twelve years of age, whose admirable talents have procured him the deserved appellation of the Infant Roscius." The public was then respectfully informed that the authorities had suspended the orders for persons being within their houses by an early hour, and that "no person coming from the theatre would be stopped until after eleven o'clock." The terms appear to have been that he was to share the house, as he had done at Belfast; and in Dublin the house held £400. His reception was of the most tumultuous kind. The Dublin audiences are as impressionable as an Italian one. The town was enraptured, though some persons of more correct taste deprecated the spectacle as unworthy of the stage; but such cavillers were overwhelmed with obloquy. He gave a round of characters, and the part of Hamlet "he learned in three mornings." Mr. Jones was eager to make arrangements for "farming" the prodigy during a number of years; but the prudent father, with Mr. Hough the prompter, who had been taken as instructor, and what is now called "advance agent," declined this proposal. He next appeared at Cork, where the nightly receipts of a wretched amphitheatre rose from ten pounds to one hundred pounds. At Glasgow he had the same success, and a person who attacked him in the papers, being discovered, was compelled to leave the city. He was received, says the manager Jackson, "with the greatest bursts of applause I ever remember to have been given by an audience. Nothing that words can express can come up to the full extent of his surprising endowments, which so strongly predominate through his infant frame." This enthusiasm seems but a type of the sort of delirium into which the kingdom was to be thrown. He declared that the boy "had been presented by Heaven," and dwelt on the "perfect and refined spirit which had been incorporated with his form previous to his birth." But at Edinburgh his reception was even more rapturous, and Lord Meadowbank addressed to him what was styled "an elegant admonitory and interesting letter," sending to him "the little work that I recommended yesterday to your perusal," and which was "by much the most valuable production of the most eminent person of your name, and on that account might merit your attention. I am convinced your mind will burn within you as you read." This was, in short, a copy of the 'Minstrel,' and it is amusing to see how either local pronunciation or national pride had lengthened "Betty" into "Beattie." He further entreated him "to form a resolution" to study the ancients—Homer, Euripides, &c. This is a good specimen of the pedantic tone of the overpraised "literary society" of Edinburgh. The last six nights here, his agent says, produced nearly £850.

He was now to appear in England, and Macready, one of the eccentric country managers, and father of the late tragedian, secured him for the Birmingham theatre. This odd being, who seems to have had some of Mr. Crummles's singularities, had employed Jackson to arrange the engagement, and was delighted at having secured the prodigy cheaply at ten pounds a night. But when the party arrived, and he saw the boy, he became eager to be let off. They, on their part, were willing to release him on payment of travelling expenses; on which, perhaps mystified by such readiness, he made a cunning proposal that sixty pounds should be deducted for the expenses of each night: after which the "house should be shared." This seemed a safe arrangement, as he probably calculated that the attraction would scarcely draw the sixty pounds. But the result turned out fortunately for Master Betty, who received fifty pounds a night instead of ten.

An "old actress," whose mother was engaged at the theatre, recently communicated some recollections of this season to a daily paper. She remembered particularly the first presentation of the boy to the Birmingham company:—

"On the morning appointed for Master Betty's first rehearsal, there was a great assembly in the green-room, and everybody evinced the utmost anxiety and curiosity to see him. He came, attended by Mr. Hough. To my childish sight he was a complete vision of beauty in the broad daylight, without the night's appliances. 'What is he like?' inquired Miss Smith, afterwards Mrs. Bartley, who succeeded Mrs. Siddons on her retirement. 'Just such a boy as you would imagine,' returned the manager; 'fair, bright-eyed, intelligent, and handsome.' Betty bowed in an elegant manner as Mr. Macready presented him and his tutor to the company. The latter kept aloof. The boy went round the room, and shook hands with all in a winning, easy manner, yet was totally devoid of either bashfulness or boldness. 'My Lord Randolph, my father, Mr. Holmes, old Norval, Glenalvon' (a very low bow). 'Allow me,' said Mrs. Glover or Mrs. Lichfield, 'as your mother, Lady Randolph, to give you a kiss,' and I quite trembled with delight as I leaned on my mother's knee, when he shook hands with her as the gentle Anna. Mr. Hough was the constant guide and companion of the Young Roscius. He was, doubtless, a clever man, and had an excellent method of instruction. My mother saw one of his marked books, with lines for the proper inflection of the voice, and instructions as to action : 'Here raise your voice—lower your voice here—put the right leg forward here—withdraw it here!'

"Master Betty made his first appearance in Birmingham, in the character of young Norval. His looks upon his entrance fascinated and riveted the attention of the audience. His youthful figure was graceful in the extreme, and the picturesque Highland costume displayed it to the utmost advantage. His features were delicate, but somewhat feminine; his eyes were a full, bright, and shining blue; his fair hair was long, and hung in ringlets over his shoulders; in the daytime those abundant tresses were confined with a comb, which still more gave the idea of a female in male costume. His first speech was heard amidst the hushed silence of the audience. It commences with 'a low-born man,' and finishes with the expression of a desire to be a soldier and 'gain a name in arms.' There was a pause, and as Lord Randolph commenced his reply he was interrupted by a tremendous burst of applause. Betty played four nights during the first week of his engagement; but on each occasion the theatre was only moderately attended. Mr. Macready began to entertain uneasy doubts as to the profit to be derived from the performances, and the actors decided that the Young Roscius was totally unattractive. His fame and reputation were, however, steadily advancing, and each succeeding night of his engagement the theatre was crowded with eager and enthusiastic spectators. The 'sensation' was potent; it had affected all sorts and conditions of people, and the rage to witness the wonderful child became universal among the inhabitants of Birmingham."

The *furore* was indeed prodigious. The hotels were crammed to overflowing: and the stagecoaches from all the district round arrived filled with persons eager to secure places at the theatre. If he excited this enthusiasm, he was also to provoke controversy, with opposition and even riot. Vehement pamphlets were issued in his praise, the most curious of which was one by Bisset, a local scribe.

The son of the country manager and the handsome boy-actor became great friends and playfellows. They used to contrive practical jokes, one of which they carried out at the house of an "influential gentleman of Birmingham," who had invited them to dine, by removing the cushions of a sofa, but leaving the cover, so that a stout old gentleman and lady, who sat down, fell through to the ground. The sketch of the old manager recalls the figure of Miss O'Neill's father, who was of the same type.

"My mother," says the 'old actress,' "acted Floranthe, the lady-love of Octavian, in 'The Mountaineers.' On Floranthe making her appearance, she was startled and confused by a rapturous burst of applause, which lasted so long that she almost felt herself a subject of ridicule; and what added to her confusion was 'Misther' Macready calling out in a broad Irish accent, 'Bow, bow! death and confusion, why don't you bow!' His

Milesian instincts were most furious when he was excited. Now my mother, who was, as I have said, very pretty, and was then in her twenty-fifth year, looked exceedingly well in male attire, yet was not vain enough to believe that her appearance was so beautiful as to excite the audience to such a rapturous expression of their admiration; consequently she did not bow, because the idea immediately occurred to her that she was mistaken for the young Roscius, which was indeed the case. The effect of this *contretemps* was that Floranthe's first scene resulted in a dead silence, and that when the boy really appeared as Octavian he was but coldly received."

The boy, who was naturally made a pet of, seems to have been engaging enough, and once wept because the manager would not allow him to act for the benefit of one of the actresses. Many stories were also told of his charity.

In this tide of success there arrived a gentleman from Drury Lane, Mr. Justice Graham, who came to pass judgment on the talents of the prodigy, and made the surprisingly meagre offer of "half a clear benefit" for seven nights' acting. This was at once declined, Manager Macready pronouncing that fifty guineas a night was the lowest that ought to be accepted. The managers of Covent Garden —Harris and Kemble—heard of the failure of this attempt, and instantly despatched a Captain Barlow to Birmingham, with *carte blanche* for terms. A rather odd engagement was then made: the boy was to appear for three nights in the last week of November, three in the first week of December, three in the last week of January, and three in the first week of February. Repenting of their slackness, the Drury Lane management then despatched an emissary with fresh offers; and, through an oversight in the Covent Garden agreement, were able to secure him for the intervening nights, for which he was not bound to the rival house. With a wish also to secure his first appearance at their house, they made him handsome offers to cancel all his provincial engagements. This he honourably refused to do; though it must be said, that the event proved that he had taken the wisest as well as the most honourable course. For all during this progress he was receiving over one hundred pounds a night, and at the same time the enthusiasm was whetting London expectancy. Bruises and torn clothes attended the operation of securing places; whilst at Manchester the confusion was so tremendous, that all applications for boxes were required to be made by letter, and, after being placed in a bag, were solemnly drawn by lot, in presence of two respectable gentlemen of the town. We learn, also, that Master Betty "enjoyed the particular notice of the Duke of Gloucester," who was commanding in that part of the country, and who was graciously pleased to express a rather barren wish that the prodigy, or "Infant Roscius," should receive a sound education. His father now received a flattering letter from the great John of Covent Garden, who, for all his devotion to what was classical, was not indifferent to what was likely to "take." He spoke of "the happiness he should soon enjoy in welcoming them to Covent Garden, and heartily congratulated the stage on the ornament and support it was to receive from Master Betty's extraordinary talents and exertions." It was hardly fair of "glorious John" to affect later to be disgusted with the raptures of the London audiences at performances which he himself had thus encouraged. At the Doncaster races, there were to be seen carriages starting for Sheffield, labelled "Theatrical Coaches, to carry six inside to see the Young Roscius;" while silver cups were presented by grateful managers.

Nothing could exceed the expectancy with which

he was waited in London. Saturday, December 1, 1804, was the day chosen for his appearance. By ten o'clock in the morning a crowd of persons was parading Bow Street and the colonnades of Covent Garden; and towards one o'clock there was a line of people at the doors of the theatre. Before evening the line was stretching in long impenetrable columns beyond Bow Street into Drury Lane. As the hour for opening drew near, the air was filled with shrieks; there was crushing and fainting. Then the crowd was admitted, and the house was filled in a few moments. Notwithstanding, there was a pressure forwards, from masses still struggling to make their way in; until a force of soldiers drew up before the doors, and saved the crowd within from being overwhelmed. As Cowper sang:

> "The theatre, too small, did suffocate
> Its squeezed contents, and more than it admitted
> Did sigh at their exclusion, and return
> Ungratified; for BETTY there, the *Boy*,
> Did strut and storm and straddle, stamp and stare,
> And show the world how GARRICK did not act."

The pit was nearly two-thirds filled by gentlemen who paid box-price, rushed in, and leaped over the balconies; when it was filled these unplaced intruders lawlessly fixed themselves in the seats of others who had secured them weeks before, and there defied the owners and their remonstrances. Box-keepers and the police were called, but, grown desperate, the intruders held their ground by main force, and with indescribable effrontery compounded for their usurpation by allowing a few ladies into the front seats. The pit was like a surging sea, and more than twenty persons, overcome by the heat and crush, had to be dragged up into the boxes, as into a boat, to be thence transported into the lobbies. As some relief, the curtain was raised about a foot, and thus allowed a current of air to blow over the pit. It was stated that some charitable ladies in the boxes passed the whole evening in fanning some exhausted gentlemen-friends in the pit. Loud shrieks would occasionally rise from the same place, and hands were seen to be lifted up, as if imploring aid and relief. At last some order was restored, and Charles Kemble came out to speak an apropos prologue, but was not listened to. He at once withdrew, and the play began. The actors were then ordered off, and the prologue called for, which was delivered in a Babel of noises. The first act of the play—which was the ranting, raging 'Barbarossa'—was got through with the same confusion, the prodigy not having to appear in it. Then came the expected moment; and Mr. Boaden, who was present, thus describes the scene:—

"At length, dressed as a slave, in white-linen pantaloons, a short, close, russet jacket, trimmed with sable, and a turban hat or cap, at the command of the tyrant, on came the desire of all eyes, —Master William Henry West Betty. With the sagacity of an old stager, I walked quietly into the house at the end of the first act, made my way into the lobby of the first circle, planted myself at the back of one of the boxes, outside, and saw him make his bow, and never stirred till the curtain fell at the end of the play. I had a good glass, and saw him perfectly. He was a fair, pleasing youth, well formed, and remarkably graceful. The first thing that struck me was, that it was passion for the profession that made him an actor; he was doing what he loved to do, and put his whole force into it. The next thing that I felt was, that he had amazing docility, and great aptitude at catching what he was taught—he could convey passions which he had never felt, nor seen in operation, but upon the stage. Grace, energy, fire, vehemence, were his own—the understanding was of a maturer brain. He seemed, however, to think all he said; and had he been taught to pronounce with accuracy, there was nothing beyond requisite for the profession."

The night was one of rapturous triumph. All his exertions were greeted with "huzzas"—a different mode of salutation from the modern cheers. The Prince of Wales, "who sat in Lady Mulgrave's box," led the applause; behind the scenes was a crowd of distinguished persons—ladies of the highest rank, who had been privileged by Mr. Brandon, the popular box-keeper; with the Lord Chief Baron, Lord Melville, and others. Mr. Colman was also present, and observed to be enthusiastic. Kemble's demeanour was characteristically reserved. "His eyes were riveted on him; that great connoisseur did not withhold his due meed of praise."

In short, a sort of delirium had now set in, and the impression produced was perhaps the most remarkable ever known on the English stage. Mrs. Mathews heard "a great man declare his belief that the boy was supernaturally gifted, and expected to see the roof of the theatre open some night and his spirit ascend"! Duchesses and other ladies of title were seen clustered round him, and their carriages were placed at his service to take him to the theatre. The King and Queen sent for him, and he was welcomed at Carlton House. When he fell sick, the street was blocked up with the carriages of fair inquirers. Bulletins were regularly issued. Northcote painted him, in one of the most ludicrously sentimental pictures that can be conceived—a languishing boy taking fire from Shakespeare's altar. The old artist told Hazlitt, with much truth, that the attraction was "his beautiful effusion of natural sensibility, which, with the graceful play of limb in youth, gave such an advantage over every one about him." "Gentleman Smith"—the Turveydrop of the stage—came up from his country place, and, with great solemnity, presented him with a ring of Garrick's, which the great actor had pledged him to give to that rare performer who acted from nature and the heart. Elliston's opinion we would be eager to know, both for the substance as well as for the form in which it was certain to be delivered. It was piquant and original, as might be expected: "Sir," he said, "my opinion of that young gentleman's talents will never transpire during my life. I have written my convictions down; they have been attested by competent witnesses, and sealed and deposited in the iron safe at my banker's, to be drawn forth and opened, with other important documents, at my death. The world will then know what Mr. Elliston thought of Master Betty." Strangest of all was a compliment from the University of Cambridge, who selected him as the subject of a prize ode.

It is amusing to see with what silent indignation the legitimate actors looked on at the success of the pigmy rival. Kemble and his greater sister were scornful and facetious. She pronounced that there was nothing in him; he was merely "a pretty child." With all their great classic *répertoire*, they now had to stand aside, while the town indulged its humour. Cooke grumbled loudly at being obliged to act with him, while the attractive Inchbald declared he was merely a clever little boy, and had she never seen boys act, would have thought him exquisite. The whole attitude, indeed, of the actors suggests one of Mr. Dickens's inimitable touches, in his account of the ruefulness with which Mr. Folair set himself to his duty of co-operating with the Phenomenon. Mrs. Jordan's was the most characteristic protest; she came into the green-room with her ringing laugh, deploring the memory of Herod. "A silly lordling," says Mrs. Mathews, "had the impertinent folly to ask

John Kemble whether he did not consider Master Betty the finest actor upon the stage." To which delicate question "glorious John," taking a pinch of snuff between his fingers and raising it slowly to his nose, with great *sang-froid* replied: "I have never, my Lord, seen the young gentleman play." Yet, as we have seen, he had addressed complimentary speeches to the prodigy, and congratulated the stage on the acquisition of such talent. Emery, Charles Kemble, Mrs. Powell, Elliston, and other actors of repute, had all to follow in the boy's train.

There can be no doubt it was a very unique and interesting entertainment, and in its way one of high merit. The proof of this is the impression left on persons of superior judgment. Charles Fox, during the excitement of the performance, went so far as to declare that he thought it as fine as Garrick's. The sober judgment of Boaden, a critic of experience, we have seen. In size, he was taller than boys of his years, and something was added to his height by artificial means; while Mrs. Lichfield, who played with him at one house, was purposely selected as being of short stature. His most successful characters were young Norval, and Selim in 'Barbarossa,' both of whom were youths;

so it really amounted to the character of a youth being presented with singular grace, intelligence, and talent by a youth—a very rare spectacle indeed. Some thought that the charm lay in his restoration of the old musical chanting that belonged to the days of Mrs. Pritchard and Mrs. Cibber. Much, too, was to be set down to his personal attractions—a soft, interesting face, a small, expressive mouth, flowing auburn hair, and a general air of intelligence.

It was only natural that the disdainful soul of Kean should decline to minister to the fame of the new idol. He later found himself at Weymouth, where Master Betty was engaged, but resolutely declined to play with him. Pressed by the manager, he fled away, and in one of his wild moods hid himself in the woods outside the town. He was later found pacing up and down in front of the theatre, bitterly execrating his fortune. "*He* has overflowing houses; *I* play to empty benches. But I know that my powers are superior to his."

The pecuniary result of this amazing tide of success was marvellous. At Drury Lane, for twenty-eight nights' performance, from December 10, 1804, to April 22, 1805, the prodigious sum of

£17,000 was taken, out of which he was paid at the rate of £100 a night for nearly the whole time. At Covent Garden he must have attracted even more money. And thus was exhibited the extraordinary phenomenon of a boy of thirteen bringing nearly £40,000 to the treasuries of two vast theatres within three months! He enjoyed, besides, the proceeds of two benefits, amounting to the handsome sum of £2500. Hamlet was the inappropriate character he chose for one of these occasions, though he took care to omit two awkward lines, singularly apropos. "Do the boys carry it always?" asks Hamlet; to whom it is replied: "Ay, that they do, my lord." In short, Mr. Boaden is inclined to believe that during this season he had almost made his fortune.

The father appears to have been eager to turn the child's talents to profit, and worked him at high pressure. He had an instinct, in which he was justified by the issue, that the *furore* would be but short-lived. Without an instant's repose, the prodigy was taken into the country for a provincial tour, during which progress the scale of his profits may be conceived from his receiving £1000 at Birmingham for thirteen nights' playing. He visited Wolverhampton, York, and Worcester.

Nearly every artist, successful in making money, is pursued with accusations of meanness and stinginess, because they do not respond to the enormous demands made upon their generosity. Garrick, Mrs. Siddons, and many more suffered cruelly from this charge. The exertions of Betty, the father, to secure all the money he could for his son naturally subjected him to such imputations. He caused a scandal by announcing a performance in Holy Week in the provinces, which drew the interference of the bishop. Moody used to tell indignantly how he had humbly asked the father of the Young Roscius to allow the boy to play for the fund for decayed actors, which would clear them from all their difficulties, and how, after six weeks' contemptuous silence, a refusal had been given. But a really shabby transaction was the treatment of Hough, the original, painstaking instructor of the boy, whose judicious assistance had been of incalculable service. This faithful ally, who had been taken from his humble post at the Belfast theatre, was now unceremoniously dismissed, and without the slightest provision. This scandalous ingratitude soon began to be talked of, and the discarded tutor, stung to fury by such neglect, threatened to lay his wrongs before the public.

The following notice was significant: "*Hough* v. *Betty*. An appeal to the judgment and candour of an impartial British public. By William Hough, late dramatic tutor to the Young Roscius. In which will be introduced a curious and truly original correspondence, previous and subsequent to Master Betty's first appearance on the stage. With notes theatrical, analytical, and explanatory. 'Blow, blow, thou winter's wind; thou art not so unkind as man's ingratitude.'" Alarmed by such a menace, the Bettys at once came to terms, and fifty pounds a year was settled on the theatrical tutor for his life.

An amusing story was told connected with one of their country tours. Stephen Kemble, whose chief title to fame, besides his relation to the greater John and Sarah, was his being "able to play Falstaff without stuffing," came to town to engage Master Betty for his theatres at Durham and Newcastle. His wife, who remained in the country, was often pressed to report his opinion of the phenomenon, but she was disinclined to do so, save in the instance of Liston, a special friend, to whom she showed a passage in her husband's letter which was to the effect that "the whole business was a humbug." Soon after, the Newcastle bills announced the prodigy, and Liston one morning finding the manager reading the box-list with great satisfaction, asked him if he thought the engagement would turn out well. "It cannot be otherwise, sir," was the reply, "*with his stupendous abilities.*" Somewhat astounded, Liston said he did not know that the manager held so high an opinion of the Young Roscius. "Sir," said Mr. Kemble emphatically, "I look upon Master Betty to be a great—nay, the greatest tragic performer that has ever appeared upon these or any other boards!" "I suppose," answered Liston, "that you except Mrs. Siddons and Mr. Kemble." "Sir," said the other, "I except nobody." Unable to resist the temptation, the actor then asked how he could reconcile such high praise with the opinion written to Mrs. Kemble. The other replied still more emphatically, "Sir, I maintain that Master Betty is the finest actor now living, and I question if he be not the finest that ever lived; for," he added, his fine eyes twinkling with humour, "*I have engaged him, sir.*"

The extravagant popularity of the Young Roscius was not destined to last beyond a couple of seasons. A hostile party presently manifested itself in the theatres, and though friends and admirers succeeded in putting it down, there was a sensible falling-off in the attraction. His benefit shrank from the triumphal £1500 to a modest £300, the average of the other performers. Still it was a compliment to find the House of Commons adjourning, on Pitt's motion, to go and see him play. His performance of Jeremy Diddler was another token of weakness. Indeed, this kind of entertainment can only flourish in extremes—mild and tempered approbation is not one of the conditions of its existence.

At last, after three or four years of hard work, during which the interest was gradually languishing, it was seen that a youth of sixteen or seventeen could no longer be considered a juvenile phenomenon. The confession of his true age at starting having effectually destroyed the chance of any of the usual theatrical fictions, in March 1808 it was announced at Bath that he was about to retire; and in July of the same year he withdrew altogether, and entered Cambridge University.

He was now to become "a gentleman!" A commission was given to him in the Shropshire Yeomanry. At the University, it was often remarked that when theatrical matters were mentioned he preserved a solemn silence, as though the subject were disagreeable. He cultivated accomplishments, and distinguished himself in the hunting-field. He contracted a taste for archery, in which he was all his life signally skilful. His eyes, however, not unnaturally, turned wistfully to the splendid triumphs of his childhood, and he was slow to believe that his success was owing to anything else but extraordinary dramatic genius. On his father's death, in 1811, he returned to the stage, making his reappearance at Bath in February 1812, receiving the handsome sum of £800 for nine nights' performance. In November he again appeared at Covent Garden at fifty guineas a night, and was able to retain his position on the stage as a clever and interesting actor for twelve years more, when in August 1824 he finally made his bow. Fifty years have passed by since that night, and it was hardly surprising that the world should have forgotten the boy that for a time extinguished the Kemble glories, and was fondled by duchesses. Nor was it astonishing that most people should have thought that years ago he had been gathered, in the almost invariable theatrical phrase, "to the tomb of all the Capulets." Putting a recently-done photograph of this interesting old gentleman beside an engraving published in the magazines of "the heaven-sent youth of 1805," the old soft and gentle air, and the outlines of the captivating features which so long ago caused such a sensation, can be recognised. He died on the 24th of August in the present year, and his story makes the last, and most curious, chapter in the ROMANCE OF THE ENGLISH STAGE.

THE END.